BIG DATA
STATISTICS, DATA MINING, ANALYTICS, AND PATTERN LEARNING

4 BOOKS IN 1

BOOK 1
BIG DATA FUNDAMENTALS: UNDERSTANDING THE BASICS
OF DATA ANALYTICS AND PROCESSING

BOOK 2
DATA MINING TECHNIQUES: EXPLORING PATTERNS AND
INSIGHTS IN BIG DATA

BOOK 3
ADVANCED DATA SCIENCE: HARNESSING MACHINE
LEARNING FOR BIG DATA ANALYSIS

BOOK 4
BIG DATA ARCHITECTURE AND SCALABILITY: DESIGNING
ROBUST SYSTEMS FOR ENTERPRISE SOLUTIONS

ROB BOTWRIGHT

1

Published by Rob Botwright
Library of Congress Cataloging-in-Publication Data
ISBN 978-1-83938-683-1
Cover design by Rizzo

Disclaimer

The contents of this book are based on extensive research and the best available historical sources. However, the author and publisher make no claims, promises, or guarantees about the accuracy, completeness, or adequacy of the information contained herein. The information in this book is provided on an "as is" basis, and the author and publisher disclaim any and all liability for any errors, omissions, or inaccuracies in the information or for any actions taken in reliance on such information. The opinions and views expressed in this book are those of the author and do not necessarily reflect the official policy or position of any organization or individual mentioned in this book. Any reference to specific people, places, or events is intended only to provide historical context and is not intended to defame or malign any group, individual, or entity. The information in this book is intended for educational and entertainment purposes only. It is not intended to be a substitute for professional advice or judgment. Readers are encouraged to conduct their own research and to seek professional advice where appropriate. Every effort has been made to obtain necessary permissions and acknowledgments for all images and other copyrighted material used in this book. Any errors or omissions in this regard are unintentional, and the author and publisher will correct them in future editions.

BOOK 1 - BIG DATA FUNDAMENTALS: UNDERSTANDING THE BASICS OF DATA ANALYTICS AND PROCESSING

BOOK 2 - DATA MINING TECHNIQUES: EXPLORING PATTERNS AND INSIGHTS IN BIG DATA

BOOK 3 - ADVANCED DATA SCIENCE: HARNESSING MACHINE LEARNING FOR BIG DATA ANALYSIS

BOOK 4 - BIG DATA ARCHITECTURE AND SCALABILITY: DESIGNING ROBUST SYSTEMS FOR ENTERPRISE SOLUTIONS

Introduction

Welcome to the "Big Data: Statistics, Data Mining, Analytics, and Pattern Learning" book bundle, a comprehensive collection designed to equip readers with the knowledge and skills needed to navigate the dynamic world of big data. In today's digital age, the sheer volume, variety, and velocity of data generated present both challenges and opportunities for organizations across industries. Harnessing the power of big data requires a deep understanding of statistical principles, data mining techniques, advanced analytics, and scalable architectures.

Book 1, "Big Data Fundamentals: Understanding the Basics of Data Analytics and Processing," lays the groundwork by providing readers with a solid understanding of the fundamental concepts and technologies driving the big data revolution. From data collection and storage to processing and analysis, this book serves as a primer for those seeking to grasp the essentials of data analytics in the context of big data.

In Book 2, "Data Mining Techniques: Exploring Patterns and Insights in Big Data," readers delve into the realm of data mining, exploring the algorithms, methodologies, and best practices for uncovering patterns and insights within large datasets. Through practical examples and case studies, readers gain insights into the application of data mining techniques across various domains, from marketing and finance to healthcare and beyond.

Building on the foundational knowledge provided in the first two books, Book 3, "Advanced Data Science: Harnessing Machine Learning for Big Data Analysis," delves into the realm of machine learning. From regression analysis to clustering and neural networks, this book explores the intricate algorithms and methodologies that drive predictive modeling and pattern recognition in big data environments.

Finally, Book 4, "Big Data Architecture and Scalability: Designing Robust Systems for Enterprise Solutions," addresses the critical considerations involved in designing scalable and resilient big data architectures. By exploring architectural patterns, scalability techniques, and fault tolerance mechanisms, readers gain insights into building robust systems capable of meeting the demands of modern enterprises.

Whether you are a beginner looking to build a solid foundation in big data analytics or an experienced professional seeking to deepen your expertise, this book bundle offers a comprehensive and insightful guide to mastering the intricacies of big data analytics and pattern learning. So, embark on this journey with us as we explore the fascinating world of big data and unlock its vast potential for innovation and discovery.

BOOK 1
BIG DATA FUNDAMENTALS
UNDERSTANDING THE BASICS OF DATA ANALYTICS AND PROCESSING

ROB BOTWRIGHT

Chapter 1: Introduction to Big Data

Understanding big data concepts is essential for navigating the increasingly data-driven world we live in. At its core, big data refers to the massive volumes of structured and unstructured data generated by various sources such as sensors, social media, and digital transactions. This data is characterized by its velocity, volume, and variety, which pose significant challenges for traditional data processing and analysis methods. To comprehend big data concepts fully, it's crucial to grasp the three Vs: volume, velocity, and variety. Volume refers to the sheer scale of data being generated, often ranging from terabytes to petabytes and beyond. Velocity pertains to the speed at which data is produced and must be processed, with real-time or near-real-time requirements becoming increasingly common. Variety encompasses the diverse types of data, including text, images, videos, and sensor data, among others. Traditional relational databases struggle to handle big data due to their limitations in scalability and processing speed. Consequently, alternative approaches such as distributed computing and NoSQL databases have emerged to address these challenges. Distributed computing frameworks like Apache Hadoop and Apache Spark enable the processing of large datasets across clusters of commodity hardware. These frameworks leverage parallel processing and fault tolerance mechanisms to analyze data efficiently. NoSQL databases, such as MongoDB and Cassandra, are designed to store and manage unstructured and semi-structured data at scale. They offer flexibility and scalability, making them suitable for big data applications where traditional relational databases fall short. In addition to volume, velocity, and variety, big data concepts also encompass the notion of veracity, referring to the accuracy and reliability of data. Veracity is critical as big data analysis relies on trustworthy data to derive meaningful insights and make informed decisions. Ensuring data quality through validation and cleansing processes is essential for maintaining veracity. Furthermore, big data concepts extend beyond technical aspects to encompass strategic and ethical considerations. Organizations must formulate clear data strategies to leverage big data effectively for business insights and innovation. This involves defining objectives, identifying relevant data sources, and establishing governance frameworks to ensure data privacy and compliance. Ethical concerns surrounding big data, such as data privacy, bias, and security, require careful consideration and mitigation strategies. Implementing access controls, anonymization techniques, and transparent data policies can help address these ethical challenges. In summary, understanding big data concepts is essential for harnessing the potential of data-driven technologies and navigating the complexities of the digital age. By grasping the fundamental principles of volume, velocity, variety, and veracity, along with strategic and ethical considerations, individuals and organizations can unlock the transformative power of big data while mitigating risks and maximizing opportunities.

The evolution of big data technologies has been marked by significant advancements and transformations over the past few decades. Initially, traditional relational database management systems (RDBMS) were the primary means of storing and processing data, but they struggled to handle the massive volumes and diverse types of data generated in the digital age. As data continued to grow exponentially, new technologies and paradigms emerged to address the scalability, speed, and complexity challenges posed by big data. One pivotal development was the introduction of distributed computing frameworks, such as Apache Hadoop, which revolutionized the way large-scale data processing was performed. Hadoop, with its distributed file system (HDFS) and MapReduce programming model, enabled the processing of massive datasets across clusters of commodity hardware, providing scalability and fault tolerance. The rise of NoSQL databases also played a crucial role in the evolution of big data technologies. Unlike traditional relational databases, NoSQL databases are designed to handle unstructured and semi-structured data types, making them well-suited for big data applications. Examples of popular NoSQL databases include MongoDB, Cassandra, and Apache CouchDB. Another key innovation in big data technology has been the emergence of real-time and stream processing frameworks. These frameworks, such as Apache Kafka and Apache Flink, enable the analysis of data streams in real-time, allowing organizations to derive insights and take actions instantaneously. In addition to processing speed, data visualization and analytics tools have also evolved to meet the demands of big data analysis. Modern analytics platforms, such as Tableau and Power BI, provide intuitive interfaces and powerful visualization capabilities, enabling users to explore and communicate insights effectively. Furthermore, advancements in cloud computing have democratized access to big data technologies, allowing organizations to leverage scalable infrastructure and services on-demand. Cloud providers like Amazon Web Services (AWS), Microsoft Azure, and Google Cloud Platform offer a wide range of big data solutions, including managed Hadoop clusters, NoSQL databases, and analytics services. As big data technologies continue to evolve, the focus is shifting towards machine learning and artificial intelligence (AI) capabilities. Machine learning algorithms and AI models are increasingly integrated into big data platforms to automate decision-making processes, uncover patterns, and generate predictive insights from data. Deploying these technologies often involves utilizing CLI commands or APIs provided by cloud service providers to provision resources, deploy applications, and manage data workflows. By embracing these advancements and leveraging the full spectrum of big data technologies, organizations can unlock the potential of their data assets and drive innovation in the digital era.

Chapter 2: The Importance of Data Analytics

The role of data analytics in decision making cannot be overstated in today's data-driven world. Data analytics encompasses a range of techniques and methodologies used to analyze and interpret data to gain insights and inform decision-making processes. By harnessing the power of data, organizations can make more informed and strategic decisions across various functions and departments. Data analytics enables businesses to uncover patterns, trends, and relationships hidden within their data, providing valuable insights into customer behavior, market dynamics, and operational performance. These insights empower decision-makers to identify opportunities, mitigate risks, and optimize processes to drive business growth and success. One of the key benefits of data analytics is its ability to facilitate evidence-based decision making. Instead of relying solely on intuition or past experiences, decision-makers can leverage data-driven insights to validate hypotheses, assess outcomes, and make informed choices. Data analytics also plays a crucial role in improving operational efficiency and effectiveness. By analyzing operational data, organizations can identify inefficiencies, bottlenecks, and areas for improvement, leading to streamlined processes and cost savings. Moreover, data analytics enables organizations to gain a deeper understanding of their customers and target audiences. By analyzing customer data, such as demographics, preferences, and purchase history, businesses can tailor their products, services, and marketing efforts to better meet customer needs and preferences. This not only enhances customer satisfaction but also drives customer loyalty and retention. In addition to improving internal operations and customer relationships, data analytics can also help organizations stay ahead of the competition. By analyzing market trends, competitor activities, and industry benchmarks, businesses can identify emerging opportunities and threats, allowing them to adapt their strategies and stay competitive in the marketplace. Furthermore, data analytics enables organizations to optimize resource allocation and strategic planning. By analyzing financial and performance data, decision-makers can allocate resources more effectively, prioritize initiatives, and optimize investments to achieve business objectives. Deploying data analytics techniques often involves using command-line interface (CLI) commands to interact with analytical tools and platforms. For example, analysts may use CLI commands to extract, transform, and load (ETL) data from various sources into a data warehouse or analytics platform. They may also use CLI commands to run analytical queries, perform statistical analysis, and generate visualizations to communicate insights effectively.

Overall, the role of data analytics in decision making is instrumental in driving organizational success and competitive advantage in today's data-driven economy. By leveraging data analytics capabilities, organizations can make smarter, more strategic decisions that drive business growth, innovation, and resilience in an increasingly complex and competitive business landscape.

The impact of data analytics on businesses is profound and far-reaching, revolutionizing how organizations operate, compete, and innovate in today's digital age. By harnessing the power of data analytics, businesses can gain valuable insights into their operations, customers, and markets, enabling them to make more informed and strategic decisions. Data analytics empowers businesses to unlock the hidden potential of their data, transforming raw data into actionable insights that drive business growth and success. Through advanced analytics techniques such as machine learning and predictive modeling, businesses can identify patterns, trends, and correlations in their data, enabling them to anticipate future trends and opportunities. This predictive capability allows businesses to proactively address challenges, mitigate risks, and capitalize on emerging opportunities, giving them a competitive edge in the marketplace. Moreover, data analytics enables businesses to optimize their operations and processes, driving efficiency, productivity, and cost savings. By analyzing operational data, businesses can identify inefficiencies, streamline workflows, and automate repetitive tasks, leading to improved performance and profitability. In addition to improving internal operations, data analytics also enhances customer relationships and experiences. By analyzing customer data, businesses can gain a deeper understanding of their customers' preferences, behaviors, and needs, allowing them to personalize products, services, and marketing efforts to better meet customer expectations. This personalized approach not only enhances customer satisfaction but also drives customer loyalty and retention, ultimately boosting revenue and profitability. Furthermore, data analytics enables businesses to gain a competitive advantage in the marketplace by providing insights into market dynamics, competitor activities, and industry trends. By analyzing market data, businesses can identify emerging trends, assess competitive threats, and capitalize on new opportunities, allowing them to stay ahead of the curve and outperform their competitors. Deploying data analytics techniques often involves using command-line interface (CLI) commands to interact with analytical tools and platforms. For example, businesses may use CLI commands to extract, transform, and load (ETL) data from various sources into a data warehouse or analytics platform. They may also use CLI commands to run analytical queries, perform statistical analysis, and generate visualizations to communicate insights effectively.

Overall, the impact of data analytics on businesses is transformative, empowering organizations to make smarter, data-driven decisions that drive innovation, growth, and competitive advantage. By leveraging the power of data analytics, businesses can unlock new opportunities, mitigate risks, and achieve their strategic objectives in an increasingly complex and competitive business landscape.

Chapter 3: Foundations of Data Processing

Data processing forms the backbone of any data-driven operation, serving as the foundation upon which insights are derived and decisions are made. At its core, data processing involves transforming raw data into a more structured format that is suitable for analysis and interpretation. This process typically involves several stages, including data collection, data cleansing, data transformation, and data integration. Data collection is the first step in the data processing pipeline, where raw data is gathered from various sources such as databases, files, sensors, and APIs. Command-line interface (CLI) commands can be used to extract data from these sources and store it in a centralized location for further processing. Once the raw data has been collected, the next step is data cleansing, where errors, inconsistencies, and missing values are identified and corrected. CLI commands can be used to perform data cleansing tasks such as removing duplicates, filling in missing values, and standardizing data formats. Data transformation is the process of converting raw data into a more structured format that is suitable for analysis. This may involve aggregating data, calculating summary statistics, or deriving new variables from existing ones. CLI commands can be used to perform data transformation tasks such as filtering, sorting, and joining datasets. Finally, data integration involves combining data from multiple sources to create a unified view of the data. This may involve merging datasets, resolving conflicts, and ensuring data consistency. CLI commands can be used to integrate data from different sources by importing, exporting, and merging datasets. Deploying data processing techniques often involves using CLI commands to interact with data processing tools and platforms. For example, analysts may use CLI commands to execute data processing pipelines using tools like Apache Spark or Apache Beam. They may also use CLI commands to schedule and monitor data processing jobs, manage dependencies, and troubleshoot issues. In summary, understanding the basics of data processing is essential for anyone working with data, from analysts and data scientists to business executives and decision-makers. By mastering the fundamentals of data processing and familiarizing themselves with CLI commands and techniques, individuals can efficiently and effectively process data to derive insights and drive business outcomes.

Data processing architectures play a crucial role in shaping how organizations handle and manage their data. These architectures define the underlying framework and infrastructure that support data processing activities, including data ingestion, storage, processing, and analysis. One of the most common data processing architectures is the batch processing architecture, which involves processing data in predefined batches at scheduled intervals. In this architecture, data is collected over a period of time and processed in bulk, typically during off-peak hours to minimize disruption to operations. CLI commands are often used to schedule and execute batch processing jobs, such as running ETL (extract, transform, load) pipelines or executing analytical queries. Another popular data processing architecture is the real-time processing architecture, which enables organizations to process and analyze data as it is generated in real-time. This architecture is well-suited for applications that require immediate insights and actions, such as fraud detection, IoT (Internet of Things) analytics, and real-time monitoring. CLI commands are used to deploy and manage real-time processing frameworks and tools, such as Apache Kafka or Apache Flink, which enable organizations to process data streams in real-time. In addition to batch and real-time processing architectures, organizations may also implement hybrid architectures that combine elements of both batch and real-time processing. In a hybrid architecture, data is processed in batches for historical analysis and reporting, while also being processed in real-time for immediate insights and actions. CLI commands are used to deploy and manage the various components of hybrid architectures, such as batch processing frameworks like Apache Hadoop and real-time processing frameworks like Apache Kafka. Deploying data processing architectures often involves deploying and configuring various components and services on cloud infrastructure or on-premises servers. CLI commands are used to provision and manage the necessary resources, such as virtual machines, storage buckets, and networking configurations. Organizations may also use containerization and orchestration technologies, such as Docker and Kubernetes, to deploy and manage data processing workloads in a scalable and efficient manner. CLI commands are used to interact with containerization and orchestration platforms, such as Docker CLI and Kubernetes CLI, to deploy and manage containerized applications and services. Overall, understanding data processing architectures and mastering CLI commands are essential skills for anyone working with data, from data engineers and architects to data analysts and scientists. By familiarizing themselves with different data processing architectures and CLI commands, individuals can effectively deploy, manage, and optimize data processing workflows to derive insights and drive business outcomes.

Chapter 4: Types of Data in Big Data Analytics

Structured data forms the backbone of many data processing and analytics workflows, providing a reliable and organized framework for storing and analyzing information. In essence, structured data refers to data that is organized into a predefined format, typically consisting of rows and columns. This format enables easy storage, retrieval, and manipulation of data, making it ideal for a wide range of applications, from databases to spreadsheets. One common example of structured data is a relational database, where data is organized into tables, with each table containing rows of data representing individual records and columns representing attributes or variables. The structured nature of relational databases allows for efficient querying and analysis using SQL (Structured Query Language) commands. For example, to retrieve data from a relational database table, one might use the SELECT command followed by the desired columns and conditions. Another example of structured data is a CSV (Comma-Separated Values) file, where data is organized into rows and columns delimited by commas. CLI commands are often used to manipulate and process CSV files, such as the cat command to display the contents of a file, the head command to view the first few lines of a file, or the awk command to extract specific columns or perform calculations. Deploying structured data involves creating and managing data structures that adhere to a predefined schema or format. In the case of relational databases, this may involve defining tables, specifying column types and constraints, and establishing relationships between tables. CLI commands are used to interact with relational database management systems (RDBMS), such as MySQL or PostgreSQL, to create, modify, and query database schemas. For example, to create a new table in a MySQL database, one might use the CREATE TABLE command followed by the table name and column definitions. Similarly, to query data from a table, one might use the SELECT command followed by the desired columns and conditions. In addition to relational databases, structured data can also be stored and managed using other data storage technologies, such as NoSQL databases and data warehouses. NoSQL databases, such as MongoDB or Cassandra, offer flexible data models that can accommodate semi-structured and unstructured data in addition to structured data. Data warehouses, such as Amazon Redshift or Google BigQuery, provide scalable storage and processing capabilities for structured data, enabling organizations to perform complex analytics and reporting tasks. CLI commands are used to interact with these data storage technologies, enabling users to manage data schemas, load data into storage, and execute queries and analytical tasks. Overall, structured data plays a fundamental role in modern data processing and analytics workflows, providing a structured and organized framework for storing, retrieving, and analyzing information. By mastering CLI commands and understanding how to deploy structured data effectively, individuals and organizations can harness the power of structured data to derive insights and make informed decisions.

Unstructured data represents a significant and growing portion of the world's data landscape, encompassing a wide range of formats and sources that do not conform to traditional relational database structures. Unlike structured data, which is organized into tables with predefined rows and columns, unstructured data lacks a formal structure, making it challenging to store, manage, and analyze using traditional data processing techniques. Common examples of unstructured data include text documents, emails, social media posts, images, videos, audio files, and sensor data. The inherent complexity and variability of unstructured data pose significant challenges for organizations seeking to extract insights and value from this vast and diverse data source. However, despite these challenges, unstructured data also presents unique opportunities for innovation and discovery. With the right tools and techniques, organizations can unlock valuable insights from unstructured data, enabling them to gain a deeper understanding of their customers, markets, and operations. One common approach to analyzing unstructured data is natural language processing (NLP), which involves using computational techniques to extract meaning and insights from text data. CLI commands can be used to deploy NLP frameworks and libraries, such as NLTK (Natural Language Toolkit) or spaCy, to perform tasks such as text parsing, sentiment analysis, named entity recognition, and topic modeling. For example, analysts may use CLI commands to tokenize and preprocess text data, train machine learning models on labeled datasets, and evaluate model performance using metrics such as accuracy or F1 score. Another approach to analyzing unstructured data is image and video processing, which involves using computer vision techniques to extract information and insights from visual data. CLI commands can be used to deploy computer vision libraries and frameworks, such as OpenCV or TensorFlow, to perform tasks such as image classification, object detection, image segmentation, and optical character recognition (OCR). For example, analysts may use CLI commands to preprocess and resize images, train convolutional neural networks (CNNs) on labeled datasets, and deploy trained models to classify or detect objects in images or videos. In addition to NLP and computer vision, unstructured data analysis may also involve techniques such as audio processing, social network analysis, and geospatial analysis, each of which requires specialized tools and expertise. CLI commands are used to deploy and manage these tools and frameworks, enabling organizations to leverage unstructured data for a wide range of applications, from customer sentiment analysis to predictive maintenance and beyond. Despite its challenges, unstructured data represents a valuable and untapped resource for organizations seeking to gain a competitive edge in today's data-driven world. By mastering CLI commands and deploying the right tools and techniques, organizations can unlock valuable insights and drive innovation using unstructured data, ultimately enabling them to make more informed decisions and achieve their business objectives.

Chapter 5: Data Collection and Storage Techniques

Data collection methods are essential for gathering the raw materials necessary for analysis and decision-making in today's data-driven world. These methods encompass a variety of techniques and tools used to collect data from various sources, ranging from traditional surveys and interviews to more modern technologies such as sensors, social media, and web scraping. Each data collection method offers its own unique advantages and challenges, making it important for organizations to carefully consider their options and choose the method or methods that best suit their needs. One common data collection method is surveys, which involve gathering information from individuals or groups through questionnaires or interviews. Surveys can be conducted in person, over the phone, via email, or through online platforms, offering flexibility and scalability for reaching diverse audiences. CLI commands can be used to deploy survey tools and platforms, such as Qualtrics or SurveyMonkey, to design, distribute, and analyze surveys efficiently. For example, researchers may use CLI commands to create survey templates, customize survey questions, and export survey responses for analysis. Another data collection method is interviews, which involve conducting structured or semi-structured conversations with individuals or groups to gather insights and information. Interviews can be conducted in person, over the phone, or via video conferencing, allowing researchers to probe deeper into topics and explore nuances that may not be captured through surveys alone. CLI commands can be used to schedule and manage interview appointments, record interview sessions, and transcribe interview recordings for analysis. For example, researchers may use CLI commands to set up calendar reminders, record audio or video interviews using tools like Zoom or Skype, and use speech-to-text software to transcribe interview recordings into text files. In addition to surveys and interviews, data collection methods also include observational studies, experiments, and secondary data analysis. Observational studies involve observing and recording behavior or phenomena in natural settings, providing valuable insights into real-world behaviors and interactions. Experiments involve manipulating variables and measuring outcomes to test hypotheses and establish causal relationships. Secondary data analysis involves reusing and analyzing data collected by others for different purposes, such as conducting meta-analyses or replicating previous studies. CLI commands can be used to manage and analyze observational data, design and execute experiments, and access and process secondary data sources. For example, researchers may use CLI commands to set up data collection instruments, monitor data streams in real-time, and perform statistical analysis on collected data. In summary, data collection methods are essential for gathering the raw materials necessary for analysis and decision-making in today's data-driven world. By mastering CLI commands and deploying the right tools and techniques, organizations can collect, manage, and analyze data efficiently and effectively, ultimately enabling them to make more informed decisions and achieve their business objectives. Storage technologies for big data play a critical role in managing the vast volumes of data generated by organizations today. These technologies encompass a wide range of solutions designed to store and organize data efficiently, securely, and cost-effectively. From traditional relational databases to distributed file systems and cloud storage services, the choice of storage technology depends on factors such as data volume, velocity, variety, and accessibility requirements. One common storage technology for big data is the distributed file system, which enables organizations to store and manage large datasets across clusters of commodity hardware. CLI commands are often used to deploy and manage distributed file systems, such as the Hadoop Distributed File System (HDFS) or the Google File System (GFS), which provide scalable and fault-tolerant storage for big data applications. For example, administrators may use CLI commands to configure storage quotas, monitor disk usage, and replicate data across multiple nodes for redundancy. Another storage technology for big data is NoSQL databases, which are designed to handle unstructured and semi-structured data types in addition to structured data. CLI commands can be used to deploy and manage NoSQL databases, such as MongoDB or Cassandra, which offer flexible data models and horizontal scalability for big data applications. For example, administrators may use CLI commands to create and configure database instances, define data schemas, and perform backups and restores. In addition to distributed file systems and NoSQL databases, organizations may also leverage cloud storage services for big data storage and management. CLI commands are used to interact with cloud storage providers, such as Amazon S3, Microsoft Azure Blob Storage, or Google Cloud Storage, to provision and manage storage resources in the cloud. For example, administrators may use CLI commands to upload and download data, manage access controls, and configure storage lifecycle policies. Furthermore, organizations may use object storage solutions for storing and managing unstructured data, such as images, videos, and documents. Object storage systems provide a scalable and cost-effective way to store large volumes of data, with built-in redundancy and durability features. CLI commands are used to interact with object storage systems, such as Amazon S3 or MinIO, to upload, download, and manage objects stored in buckets or containers. In summary, storage technologies for big data are essential for organizations seeking to manage and analyze large volumes of data efficiently and effectively. By mastering CLI commands and deploying the right storage solutions, organizations can ensure that their data is stored securely, accessible when needed, and scalable to meet the demands of their business operations.

Chapter 6: Data Cleaning and Preprocessing Essentials

Data cleaning techniques are fundamental processes in the realm of data management and analysis, serving as the foundation for ensuring data quality and reliability. In today's data-driven world, where organizations rely heavily on data for decision-making and strategic planning, the importance of data cleaning cannot be overstated. Data cleaning involves identifying and rectifying errors, inconsistencies, and anomalies in datasets to improve accuracy, completeness, and consistency. These errors can arise from various sources, including data entry mistakes, system glitches, or sensor malfunctions, and can significantly impact the validity and reliability of analytical results. Therefore, employing effective data cleaning techniques is essential for ensuring that data-driven decisions are based on reliable and trustworthy information.

One common data cleaning technique is data deduplication, which involves identifying and removing duplicate records or observations from a dataset. CLI commands can be used to implement data deduplication processes, such as sorting data based on unique identifiers and removing duplicate entries using tools like awk or sed. For example, analysts may use CLI commands to identify duplicate customer records in a CRM database and merge or remove duplicate entries to ensure data integrity.

Another important data cleaning technique is missing data imputation, which involves estimating or predicting missing values in a dataset based on available information. CLI commands can be used to perform missing data imputation using statistical methods or machine learning algorithms. For example, analysts may use CLI commands to replace missing values in a dataset with the mean, median, or mode of the corresponding variable, or to train predictive models to estimate missing values based on other variables in the dataset.

In addition to deduplication and missing data imputation, data cleaning also involves identifying and correcting inconsistencies and outliers in datasets. CLI commands can be used to detect inconsistencies and outliers using statistical methods or data visualization techniques. For example, analysts may use CLI commands to calculate summary statistics for variables in a dataset and identify data points that fall outside a certain range or distribution. They may also use CLI commands to create histograms, box plots, or scatter plots to visualize the distribution of data and identify potential outliers.

Furthermore, data cleaning may also involve standardizing data formats and units to ensure consistency and comparability across different datasets. CLI commands can be used to convert data into standard formats or units using tools like awk or sed. For example, analysts may use CLI commands to convert dates into a consistent format or to convert measurements from different units (e.g., inches to centimeters) for analysis.

Moreover, data cleaning techniques may also include correcting errors in categorical variables, such as typos or misspellings in text data. CLI commands can be used to identify and correct errors in categorical variables using techniques like fuzzy matching or regular expressions. For example, analysts may use CLI commands to search for and replace misspelled words or inconsistent labels in a dataset using regular expressions.

In summary, data cleaning techniques are essential processes for ensuring data quality and reliability in data management and analysis workflows. By employing effective data cleaning techniques, organizations can improve the accuracy, completeness, and consistency of their datasets, ultimately leading to more reliable and trustworthy insights and decisions. CLI commands play a crucial role in implementing data cleaning techniques, enabling analysts to automate and streamline the data cleaning process efficiently and effectively.

Preprocessing steps for analysis are critical components of any data analysis workflow, serving to prepare raw data for further exploration and modeling. These steps involve cleaning, transforming, and preparing data to ensure its quality, consistency, and suitability for analysis. In today's data-driven world, where organizations rely heavily on data to make informed decisions and gain valuable insights, the importance of preprocessing cannot be overstated. Effective preprocessing can significantly impact the accuracy and reliability of analytical results, ultimately leading to more informed decision-making and improved business outcomes.

One of the first preprocessing steps is data cleaning, which involves identifying and rectifying errors, inconsistencies, and missing values in datasets. CLI commands are often used to implement data cleaning processes, such as removing duplicates, imputing missing values, and correcting errors. For example, analysts may use CLI commands to remove duplicate records from a dataset using tools like awk or sed, or to impute missing values using statistical methods or machine learning algorithms.

Another important preprocessing step is data transformation, which involves converting raw data into a more suitable format for analysis. CLI commands can be used to perform data transformation tasks such as aggregating, summarizing, and normalizing data. For example, analysts may use CLI commands to aggregate sales data by month or year, calculate summary statistics such as mean or median, or normalize data by scaling it to a common range.

In addition to data cleaning and transformation, preprocessing steps may also include feature engineering, which involves creating new variables or features from existing ones to improve model performance. CLI commands can be used to perform feature engineering tasks such as creating dummy variables, binning continuous variables, or extracting information from text or date variables. For example, analysts may use CLI commands to create dummy variables for categorical variables using tools like awk or sed, or to extract day of the week or month from date variables using regular expressions.

Furthermore, preprocessing steps may also involve data scaling and normalization, which involves scaling numerical variables to a common range or distribution to improve model performance and stability. CLI commands can be used to scale and normalize data using techniques such as min-max scaling or z-score normalization. For example, analysts may use CLI commands to scale numerical variables to a range of 0 to 1 using the min-max scaling formula or to standardize variables to have a mean of 0 and standard deviation of 1 using the z-score normalization formula.

Moreover, preprocessing steps may also include data encoding, which involves converting categorical variables into a numerical format suitable for analysis. CLI commands can be used to encode categorical variables using techniques such as one-hot encoding or label encoding. For example, analysts may use CLI commands to create dummy variables for categorical variables using tools like awk or sed, or to encode categorical variables as numerical values using label encoding.

In summary, preprocessing steps for analysis are essential processes for preparing raw data for exploration and modeling. By employing effective preprocessing techniques, organizations can improve the quality, consistency, and suitability of their datasets for analysis, ultimately leading to more accurate and reliable insights and decisions. CLI commands play a crucial role in implementing preprocessing steps, enabling analysts to automate and streamline the preprocessing process efficiently and effectively. Additionally, preprocessing steps may involve outlier detection and handling, which involves identifying and addressing data points that deviate significantly from the rest of the dataset. CLI commands can be used to detect outliers using statistical methods or data visualization techniques. For example, analysts may use CLI commands to calculate summary statistics such as mean and standard deviation and identify data points that fall outside a certain range or distribution.

Furthermore, preprocessing may also include data sampling, which involves selecting a subset of data points from a larger dataset for analysis. CLI commands can be used to perform data sampling tasks such as random sampling, stratified sampling, or oversampling. For example, analysts may use CLI commands to randomly select a certain percentage of records from a dataset using tools like awk or sed.

Moreover, preprocessing steps may involve data partitioning, which involves dividing a dataset into training, validation, and test sets for model development and evaluation. CLI commands can be used to partition data using techniques such as random splitting or stratified splitting. For example, analysts may use CLI commands to split a dataset into training and test sets with a specified ratio using tools like awk or sed.

In addition to the above preprocessing steps, data preprocessing may also involve text preprocessing for natural language processing (NLP) tasks. Text preprocessing steps may include tokenization, stemming, lemmatization, and stop word removal. CLI commands can be used to perform text preprocessing tasks using tools like NLTK or spaCy. For example, analysts may use CLI commands to tokenize text data into individual words or sentences, remove stop words, and perform stemming or lemmatization to normalize word forms.

Furthermore, preprocessing steps may also involve scaling and normalizing image data for computer vision tasks. Image preprocessing techniques may include resizing, cropping, and normalization. CLI commands can be used to perform image preprocessing tasks using tools like OpenCV or TensorFlow. For example, analysts may use CLI commands to resize images to a standard size, crop images to focus on relevant regions of interest, and normalize pixel values to a common range.

Overall, preprocessing steps are essential for preparing raw data for analysis and modeling tasks. By employing effective preprocessing techniques, organizations can improve the quality, consistency, and suitability of their datasets for analysis, ultimately leading to more accurate and reliable insights and decisions. CLI commands play a crucial role in implementing preprocessing steps, enabling analysts to automate and streamline the preprocessing process efficiently and effectively.

Chapter 7: Analytical Tools and Techniques

Analytical tools are indispensable assets in the arsenal of data scientists, analysts, and decision-makers alike. These tools empower users to extract insights, uncover patterns, and derive actionable intelligence from vast volumes of data. In today's data-driven world, where organizations are inundated with information from diverse sources, the ability to harness the power of analytical tools is paramount to gaining a competitive edge and driving innovation.

CLI commands play a pivotal role in the deployment and utilization of analytical tools, providing users with a powerful interface to interact with and manipulate data. Command-line interfaces enable users to execute commands directly from a terminal window, allowing for seamless integration with analytical tools and workflows. For instance, when working with popular data processing frameworks such as Apache Spark or Hadoop, CLI commands are used to launch jobs, monitor job status, and manage cluster resources.

One of the most widely used analytical tools is Python, a versatile programming language renowned for its simplicity and flexibility. Python boasts a rich ecosystem of libraries and frameworks tailored for data analysis and machine learning, including NumPy, Pandas, Matplotlib, and Scikit-learn. CLI commands are often used to install Python packages, manage virtual environments, and execute Python scripts. For example, users can use the pip command to install Python packages from the Python Package Index (PyPI) or create isolated Python environments using virtualenv.

Another popular analytical tool is R, a programming language and environment specifically designed for statistical computing and graphics. R offers a comprehensive set of packages for data manipulation, visualization, and modeling, making it a favorite among statisticians and data analysts. CLI commands can be used to install R packages, update package dependencies, and execute R scripts. For example, users can utilize the install.packages() function in R to install packages from the Comprehensive R Archive Network (CRAN) or use the Rscript command to execute R scripts from the command line.

In addition to programming languages, graphical user interface (GUI) tools also play a vital role in data analysis and visualization. GUI-based analytical tools offer intuitive interfaces for exploring data, creating visualizations, and building predictive models without requiring extensive programming knowledge. CLI commands may still be utilized to launch and manage these GUI tools, particularly in cases where automation or scripting is necessary. For example, users can use CLI commands to automate the generation of reports or dashboards using GUI tools like Tableau or Power BI.

Furthermore, cloud-based analytical platforms have emerged as a popular choice for organizations seeking scalable and cost-effective solutions for data analysis. Platforms such as Google Cloud Platform (GCP), Amazon Web Services (AWS), and Microsoft Azure offer a plethora of analytical tools and services, ranging from data storage and processing to machine learning and artificial intelligence. CLI commands are instrumental in managing cloud resources, deploying analytical services, and automating workflows on these platforms. For instance, users can utilize the gcloud command-line tool on GCP or the aws command-line interface on AWS to interact with cloud services, provision resources, and execute analytical tasks.

Moreover, open-source analytical tools and frameworks have democratized access to advanced analytics capabilities, allowing organizations of all sizes to leverage cutting-edge technologies without the burden of licensing fees or vendor lock-in. Tools such as Apache Spark, TensorFlow, and Jupyter Notebooks have gained widespread adoption in the data science community, enabling users to tackle complex analytical tasks with ease. CLI commands are integral to deploying and managing these open-source tools, whether on local machines or distributed computing clusters. For example, users can use the spark-submit command to submit Spark jobs or the pip command to install TensorFlow on their systems.

In summary, analytical tools are indispensable assets for extracting insights and driving innovation in today's data-driven world. Whether through programming languages like Python and R, GUI-based tools, cloud-based platforms, or open-source frameworks, the ability to harness the power of analytical tools is essential for organizations seeking to gain a competitive edge and unlock the full potential of their data. CLI commands serve as a gateway to deploying and managing these tools, providing users with the flexibility and control needed to tackle complex analytical challenges effectively. By mastering CLI commands and embracing analytical tools, organizations can unlock new opportunities for growth, innovation, and success in the digital age.

Analytical techniques are indispensable tools in the realm of data analysis, enabling organizations to extract meaningful insights and make informed decisions from their data. From descriptive statistics to advanced machine learning algorithms, a diverse array of techniques exists to analyze and interpret data across various domains and industries. In this section, we will explore some of the most commonly used analytical techniques and how they can be deployed effectively using command-line interface (CLI) commands.

Descriptive Statistics:

Descriptive statistics provide a summary of the key characteristics of a dataset, such as central tendency, dispersion, and shape. They serve as the foundation for understanding the underlying distribution of data and identifying potential patterns or outliers. To calculate descriptive statistics using CLI commands, we can leverage statistical software packages like R or Python. For example, in R, we can use the summary() function to generate summary statistics for a dataset:

cssCopy code

```
summary(data)
```

This command will output a summary table containing key descriptive statistics such as mean, median, minimum, maximum, and quartiles for each variable in the dataset.

Exploratory Data Analysis (EDA):

Exploratory data analysis (EDA) involves visually exploring and summarizing data to identify trends, patterns, and relationships. CLI commands can be used to generate visualizations such as histograms, scatter plots, and box plots to gain insights into the underlying structure of the data. In Python, we can use libraries like Matplotlib and Seaborn to create various types of plots. For example, to create a histogram of a numeric variable in Python, we can use the following command:

kotlinCopy code

```
import matplotlib.pyplot as plt
plt.hist(data['variable'], bins=10) plt.xlabel('Variable')
plt.ylabel('Frequency') plt.title('Histogram of
Variable') plt.show()
```

This command will generate a histogram displaying the distribution of values for the specified variable.

Regression Analysis:

Regression analysis is a statistical technique used to model the relationship between one or more independent variables and a dependent variable. It is commonly used for predictive modeling and hypothesis testing. To perform regression analysis using CLI commands, we can use statistical software packages like R or Python. In R, we can use the lm() function to fit a linear regression model to our data:

scssCopy code

```
model        <-        lm(dependent_variable       ~
independent_variable1    +    independent_variable2,
data=data) summary(model)
```

This command will fit a linear regression model to the data, with the specified dependent variable and independent variables, and output a summary table containing the model coefficients, standard errors, t-values, and p-values.

Cluster Analysis:

Cluster analysis is a technique used to group similar objects or observations together based on their characteristics. It is commonly used for segmentation and pattern recognition. To perform cluster analysis using CLI commands, we can use clustering algorithms such as k-means or hierarchical clustering. In Python, we can use libraries like scikit-learn to implement these algorithms. For example, to perform k-means clustering in Python, we can use the following command:

scssCopy code

```
from sklearn.cluster import KMeans kmeans =
KMeans(n_clusters=3) kmeans.fit(data) clusters =
kmeans.predict(data)
```

This command will fit a k-means clustering model to the data, with the specified number of clusters, and assign each observation to a cluster based on its proximity to the cluster centroids.

Classification:

Classification is a supervised learning technique used to predict the class label of new observations based on their features. It is commonly used for tasks such as spam detection, image recognition, and sentiment analysis. To perform classification using CLI commands, we can use classification algorithms such as logistic regression, decision trees, or support vector machines. In Python, we can use libraries like scikit-learn to implement these algorithms. For example, to fit a logistic regression model to our data in Python, we can use the following command:

scssCopy code

```
from sklearn.linear_model import LogisticRegression
model = LogisticRegression() model.fit(X_train,
y_train)
```

This command will fit a logistic regression model to the training data, with the specified independent variables (X_train) and dependent variable (y_train).

In summary, analytical techniques are essential tools for extracting insights and making informed decisions from data. From descriptive statistics to advanced machine learning algorithms, these techniques enable organizations to uncover valuable insights and gain a competitive edge. By leveraging CLI commands and statistical software packages like R and Python, analysts can deploy these techniques effectively and efficiently, empowering them to extract actionable insights from their data and drive business success.

Chapter 8: Introduction to Statistical Analysis

Statistical concepts form the foundation of data analysis, providing essential tools and techniques for understanding, summarizing, and interpreting data. In this section, we will explore some fundamental statistical concepts and how they can be applied using command-line interface (CLI) commands or statistical software packages.

Descriptive Statistics:

Descriptive statistics are used to summarize and describe the main features of a dataset. They provide insights into the central tendency, dispersion, and shape of the data distribution. One common descriptive statistic is the mean, which represents the average value of a dataset. To calculate the mean using CLI commands, we can use tools like R or Python. In R, the mean() function can be used as follows:

```scss
scssCopy code
mean(data)
```

This command will calculate the mean of the specified variable in the dataset.

Another important descriptive statistic is the standard deviation, which measures the spread or dispersion of the data around the mean. In R, the sd() function can be used to calculate the standard deviation:

```scss
scssCopy code
sd(data)
```

This command will compute the standard deviation of the specified variable in the dataset.

Inferential Statistics:

Inferential statistics are used to make predictions or inferences about a population based on a sample of data. One common inferential statistic is the confidence interval, which provides a range of values within which the true population parameter is likely to fall with a certain level of confidence. To calculate confidence intervals using CLI commands, we can use statistical software packages like R or Python. In R, the t.test() function can be used to calculate confidence intervals for the mean:

kotlinCopy code

```
t.test(data, conf.level=0.95)
```

This command will compute a 95% confidence interval for the mean of the specified variable in the dataset.

Hypothesis Testing:

Hypothesis testing is a statistical method used to make decisions about a population based on sample data. It involves formulating null and alternative hypotheses and using statistical tests to determine whether there is enough evidence to reject the null hypothesis. One common hypothesis test is the t-test, which is used to compare the means of two groups. In R, the t.test() function can be used to perform a t-test:

scssCopy code

```
t.test(data1, data2)
```

This command will conduct a t-test to compare the means of the two specified datasets.

Another commonly used hypothesis test is the chi-squared test, which is used to determine whether there is a significant association between two categorical variables. In R, the chisq.test() function can be used to perform a chi-squared test:

cssCopy code

```
chisq.test(table)
```

This command will conduct a chi-squared test on the specified contingency table.

Correlation and Regression:

Correlation and regression are statistical techniques used to measure and analyze relationships between variables. Correlation measures the strength and direction of the linear relationship between two continuous variables, while regression predicts the value of one variable based on the value of another variable. In R, the cor.test() function can be used to calculate the correlation coefficient and test for correlation significance:

wasmCopy code

```
cor.test(data$variable1, data$variable2)
```

This command will compute the correlation coefficient between the two specified variables in the dataset.

Regression analysis can be performed using the lm() function in R:

scssCopy code

```
model            <-            lm(dependent_variable        ~
independent_variable, data=data) summary(model)
```
This command will fit a linear regression model to the data and output a summary of the model results.

Probability Distributions:

Probability distributions describe the likelihood of different outcomes in a random process. Common probability distributions include the normal distribution, binomial distribution, and Poisson distribution. In R, probability distributions can be visualized using functions like plot() and density().

scssCopy code

```
plot(density(data))
```

This command will create a density plot of the specified variable in the dataset.

In summary, basic statistical concepts are essential for understanding and analyzing data. By applying these concepts using CLI commands or statistical software packages like R or Python, analysts can gain valuable insights into their data and make informed decisions. Whether calculating descriptive statistics, performing hypothesis tests, or analyzing relationships between variables, a solid understanding of statistical concepts is crucial for effective data analysis and interpretation.

Statistical methods are essential tools for analyzing and interpreting data across various domains and industries. From descriptive statistics to inferential techniques, these methods enable researchers, analysts, and decision-makers to uncover insights, test hypotheses, and make informed decisions based on data evidence. In this section, we will explore some of the key statistical methods used in data analysis and how they can be applied using command-line interface (CLI) commands or statistical software packages.

Descriptive Statistics:

Descriptive statistics provide summaries and visualizations that help to understand the main features of a dataset. These statistics include measures of central tendency, such as mean, median, and mode, as well as measures of dispersion, such as standard deviation and range. To compute descriptive statistics using CLI commands, we can utilize tools like R or Python. For example, in R, the summary() function can be used to generate summary statistics for a dataset:

cssCopy code

```
summary(data)
```

This command will output summary statistics, including mean, median, minimum, maximum, and quartiles, for each variable in the dataset.

In Python, the describe() method can be used to obtain similar summary statistics:

scssCopy code

```
print(data.describe())
```

This command will provide summary statistics for numeric variables in the dataset, including count, mean, standard deviation, minimum, maximum, and percentiles.

Inferential Statistics:

Inferential statistics are used to make predictions or inferences about a population based on sample data. These methods include hypothesis testing, confidence intervals, and regression analysis. To perform inferential statistics using CLI commands, we can use statistical software packages like R or Python. For example, in R, the t.test() function can be used to conduct a t-test:

wasmCopy code

```
t.test(data$group1, data$group2)
```

This command will perform a t-test to compare the means of two groups in the dataset and determine whether they are significantly different from each other.

In Python, the ttest_ind() function from the scipy.stats module can be used to conduct a t-test:

pythonCopy code

```
from scipy.stats import ttest_ind t_stat, p_value = ttest_ind(group1, group2) print("t-statistic:", t_stat) print("p-value:", p_value)
```

This command will calculate the t-statistic and p-value for the t-test comparing the means of two groups.

Regression Analysis:

Regression analysis is a statistical method used to model the relationship between one or more independent variables and a dependent variable. It is commonly used for prediction and hypothesis testing. To perform regression analysis using CLI commands, we can use statistical software packages like R or

Python. For example, in R, the lm() function can be used to fit a linear regression model:

scssCopy code

```
model <- lm(dependent_variable ~ independent_variable1 + independent_variable2, data=data) summary(model)
```

This command will fit a linear regression model to the data, with the specified dependent variable and independent variables, and output a summary of the model results.

In Python, the statsmodels library can be used to perform regression analysis:

scssCopy code

```
import statsmodels.api as sm model = sm.OLS(dependent_variable, sm.add_constant(independent_variables)).fit() print(model.summary())
```

This command will fit an ordinary least squares (OLS) regression model to the data and output a summary of the model results.

Time Series Analysis:

Time series analysis is a statistical method used to analyze data collected over time and identify patterns or trends. It is commonly used in fields such as finance, economics, and environmental science. To perform time series analysis using CLI commands, we can use statistical software packages like R or Python. For example, in R, the forecast package can be used to fit time series models:

scssCopy code

```
library(forecast)      model      <-      auto.arima(data)
plot(forecast(model))
```

This command will fit an automatic ARIMA model to the time series data and generate a forecast plot.

In Python, the statsmodels library can be used to perform time series analysis:

scssCopy code

```
import    statsmodels.api    as    sm    model    =
sm.tsa.ARIMA(data,    order=(p,    d,    q))    results    =
model.fit() print(results.summary())
```

This command will fit an autoregressive integrated moving average (ARIMA) model to the time series data and output a summary of the model results.

In summary, statistical methods are powerful tools for analyzing and interpreting data. From descriptive statistics to inferential techniques, regression analysis to time series analysis, these methods enable researchers and analysts to uncover insights, test hypotheses, and make informed decisions based on data evidence. By leveraging CLI commands and statistical software packages like R or Python, analysts can deploy these methods effectively and efficiently, empowering them to extract valuable insights from their data and drive business success.

Top of Form

Chapter 9: Data Visualization Fundamentals

Data visualization plays a crucial role in modern data analysis, providing a powerful means to communicate insights, trends, and patterns in data effectively. As organizations grapple with ever-increasing volumes of data, the ability to visualize information in a clear and intuitive manner has become essential for making informed decisions and driving strategic initiatives. In this section, we will explore the importance of data visualization and how it can be deployed using command-line interface (CLI) commands or specialized visualization tools.

Visualization is a fundamental aspect of the human cognitive process, enabling us to process and interpret complex information more easily than raw data. By presenting data visually through charts, graphs, and dashboards, analysts can convey key messages and insights to stakeholders in a compelling and understandable way. CLI commands can be used to generate visualizations using tools like R, Python, or specialized visualization libraries.

For example, in R, the ggplot2 package provides a versatile framework for creating a wide range of visualizations, including scatter plots, bar charts, and histograms. To create a scatter plot of two variables in R, we can use the following command:

scssCopy code

```
library(ggplot2)    ggplot(data,    aes(x=variable1,
y=variable2)) + geom_point()
```
This command will generate a scatter plot of the specified variables in the dataset, with points representing individual data points.

In Python, the matplotlib and Seaborn libraries are commonly used for data visualization. To create a bar chart of categorical data in Python using Seaborn, we can use the following command:

kotlinCopy code

```
import seaborn as sns sns.countplot(x='category',
data=data)
```
This command will generate a bar chart showing the count of observations in each category.

Data visualization is not only valuable for exploring and understanding data but also for communicating findings and insights to others. Visualizations enable stakeholders to grasp complex information quickly and make data-driven decisions with confidence. Whether presenting insights to executives, sharing findings with colleagues, or engaging with customers, compelling visualizations can enhance communication and foster understanding.

Moreover, data visualization can reveal patterns and trends in data that may not be apparent from raw numbers alone. By plotting data over time, analysts can identify seasonality, trends, and anomalies that may inform strategic decision-making. CLI commands can be used to create time series plots, line charts, or heatmaps to visualize temporal patterns in data.

For example, in Python, the pandas library can be used to manipulate time series data, and the matplotlib library can be used to create visualizations. To create a line chart of time series data in Python, we can use the following command:

kotlinCopy code

```
import matplotlib.pyplot as plt data['date'] = pd.to_datetime(data['date']) plt.plot(data['date'], data['value']) plt.xlabel('Date') plt.ylabel('Value') plt.title('Time Series Plot') plt.show()
```

This command will generate a line chart showing the value of the variable over time.

Furthermore, data visualization can help identify outliers, errors, or inconsistencies in data that may require further investigation. By visualizing data distributions, analysts can spot anomalies that may indicate data quality issues or errors in data collection. CLI commands can be used to create box plots, histograms, or scatter plots to visualize data distributions and identify outliers.

For example, in R, the ggplot2 package can be used to create a box plot of a numeric variable in the dataset. To create a box plot in R, we can use the following command:

scssCopy code

```
ggplot(data, aes(x=variable)) + geom_boxplot()
```

This command will generate a box plot showing the distribution of the specified variable in the dataset.

In summary, data visualization is a critical component of modern data analysis, enabling analysts to explore, understand, and communicate insights effectively. By leveraging CLI commands and specialized visualization tools, analysts can create compelling visualizations that reveal patterns, trends, and outliers in data, facilitating informed decision-making and driving business success. Whether presenting insights to stakeholders, identifying anomalies in data, or uncovering hidden patterns, data visualization is an indispensable tool for extracting value from data and unlocking its full potential.

Visualization techniques and tools are indispensable components of modern data analysis, enabling analysts to explore, understand, and communicate insights effectively. In this section, we will delve into various visualization techniques and the tools available to deploy them, including command-line interface (CLI) commands or specialized visualization software. Scatter Plots: Scatter plots are a fundamental visualization technique used to visualize the relationship between two variables. They are particularly useful for identifying patterns, trends, and correlations in data. To create a scatter plot using CLI commands in R, we can utilize the ggplot2 package:

```
scssCopy code
library(ggplot2)     ggplot(data,     aes(x=variable1,
y=variable2)) + geom_point()
```

This command will generate a scatter plot of the specified variables in the dataset, with points representing individual data points.

Bar Charts: Bar charts are effective for visualizing categorical data and comparing the frequencies or proportions of different categories. They provide a straightforward way to convey information and identify trends across categories. To create a bar chart using CLI commands in Python with the Seaborn library:

kotlinCopy code

```
import seaborn as sns sns.countplot(x='category', data=data)
```

This command will generate a bar chart showing the count of observations in each category.

Line Charts: Line charts are commonly used to visualize trends over time or across ordered categories. They are particularly effective for displaying time series data and highlighting temporal patterns. To create a line chart using CLI commands in Python with the Matplotlib library:

kotlinCopy code

```
import matplotlib.pyplot as plt plt.plot(data['date'], data['value']) plt.xlabel('Date') plt.ylabel('Value') plt.title('Time Series Plot') plt.show()
```

This command will generate a line chart showing the value of the variable over time.

Heatmaps: Heatmaps are useful for visualizing patterns and relationships in two-dimensional data, such as correlations or spatial distributions. They provide a color-coded representation of data values, making it easy to identify clusters or gradients. To create a heatmap using CLI commands in Python with the Seaborn library:

kotlinCopy code

```
import seaborn as sns sns.heatmap(data.corr(),
annot=True, cmap='coolwarm')
```

This command will generate a heatmap showing the correlation matrix of the variables in the dataset, with annotations displaying the correlation coefficients.

Histograms: Histograms are used to visualize the distribution of a single continuous variable. They provide insights into the shape, center, and spread of the data distribution. To create a histogram using CLI commands in R:

bashCopy code

```
hist(data$variable, breaks=10, main='Histogram of
Variable', xlab='Value', ylab='Frequency')
```

This command will generate a histogram of the specified variable in the dataset, with the number of bins specified by the breaks argument.

Box Plots: Box plots are effective for visualizing the distribution of a continuous variable across different categories or groups. They provide insights into the central tendency, spread, and variability of the data within each category. To create a box plot using CLI commands in R with the ggplot2 package:

scssCopy code

```
library(ggplot2)      ggplot(data,      aes(x=category,
y=variable)) + geom_boxplot()
```

This command will generate a box plot of the specified variable, grouped by category.

Pie Charts: Pie charts are useful for visualizing the composition of a categorical variable as a proportion of the whole. They provide a simple and intuitive way to compare the relative sizes of different categories. To create a pie chart using CLI commands in Python with the Matplotlib library:

kotlinCopy code

```
import matplotlib.pyplot as plt
plt.pie(data['category'].value_counts(),
labels=data['category'].unique(), autopct='%1.1f%%')
plt.title('Pie Chart of Category') plt.show()
```

This command will generate a pie chart showing the distribution of the categories in the dataset as a percentage of the whole.

In summary, visualization techniques and tools are essential for exploring, understanding, and communicating insights from data. By leveraging CLI commands or specialized visualization software, analysts can create compelling visualizations that reveal patterns, trends, and relationships in data, enabling informed decision-making and driving business success. Whether creating scatter plots, bar charts, line charts, or heatmaps, the ability to deploy visualization techniques effectively is a valuable skill for any data analyst or researcher.

Chapter 10: Real-World Applications of Big Data

Big Data has emerged as a transformative force in the healthcare industry, revolutionizing how medical data is collected, analyzed, and utilized to improve patient outcomes, optimize operations, and drive innovation. In this section, we will delve into the role of Big Data in healthcare, exploring its applications, benefits, challenges, and deployment techniques using command-line interface (CLI) commands or specialized tools.

Electronic Health Records (EHR): Electronic Health Records (EHR) have become a cornerstone of modern healthcare systems, providing a comprehensive digital record of a patient's medical history, diagnoses, treatments, and outcomes. CLI commands can be used to extract and analyze data from EHR systems, enabling healthcare providers to gain insights into patient populations, identify trends, and personalize treatment plans.

For example, in SQL, we can use the SELECT statement to query data from an EHR database:

sqlCopy code

```
SELECT * FROM patients WHERE diagnosis = 'diabetes';
```

This command will retrieve all patient records with a diagnosis of diabetes from the database.

Predictive Analytics: Predictive analytics leverages Big Data to forecast future events or outcomes based on historical data patterns. In healthcare, predictive analytics can be used to identify patients at risk of developing certain conditions, predict disease progression, or optimize treatment strategies. CLI commands can be used to train predictive models and make predictions using statistical software packages like R or Python.

For instance, in Python, we can use the scikit-learn library to train a predictive model:

scssCopy code

```
from sklearn.model_selection import train_test_split
from sklearn.linear_model import LogisticRegression
X_train, X_test, y_train, y_test = train_test_split(X, y, test_size=0.2, random_state=42) model = LogisticRegression() model.fit(X_train, y_train) predictions = model.predict(X_test)
```

This command will split the data into training and testing sets, train a logistic regression model on the training data, and make predictions on the testing data.

Remote Patient Monitoring: Remote Patient Monitoring (RPM) uses connected devices and sensors to collect real-time health data from patients outside of traditional healthcare settings. This data can include vital signs, medication adherence, and activity levels, allowing healthcare providers to monitor patient health remotely and intervene proactively when necessary. CLI commands can be used to process and analyze the vast amounts of data generated by RPM devices, enabling clinicians to detect early warning signs and prevent complications. For example, in R, we can use the dplyr package to filter and summarize RPM data:

scssCopy code

```
library(dplyr) rpm_data %>% filter(patient_id == '123') %>% summarize(avg_heart_rate = mean(heart_rate))
```

This command will filter the RPM data for a specific patient and calculate the average heart rate over the monitoring period.

Precision Medicine: Precision medicine aims to tailor medical treatment and interventions to individual patients based on their unique genetic, environmental, and lifestyle factors. Big Data plays a crucial role in precision medicine by enabling researchers to analyze large-scale genomic data, identify genetic markers of disease, and develop targeted therapies. CLI commands can be used to process and analyze genomic data, facilitating the discovery of personalized treatment approaches.

For instance, in Python, we can use the pandas library to manipulate genomic data:

javaCopy code

```
import pandas as pd genomic_data = pd.read_csv('genomic_data.csv')
```

This command will read genomic data from a CSV file into a pandas DataFrame for further analysis.

Healthcare Fraud Detection: Healthcare fraud is a significant issue that costs billions of dollars each year and compromises patient safety and quality of care.

Big Data analytics can help healthcare organizations detect and prevent fraudulent activities by analyzing claims data, provider billing patterns, and patient records for suspicious patterns or anomalies. CLI commands can be used to apply machine learning algorithms to identify fraudulent transactions and flag them for further investigation.

For example, in R, we can use the randomForest package to train a fraud detection model:

scssCopy code

```
library(randomForest) model <- randomForest(fraud ~ ., data=claims_data)
```

This command will train a random forest model to predict fraudulent claims based on features in the claims data.

In summary, Big Data has the potential to revolutionize healthcare by enabling data-driven decision-making, personalized treatment approaches, and improved patient outcomes. By leveraging CLI commands and specialized analytics tools, healthcare organizations can harness the power of Big Data to enhance patient care, optimize operations, and drive innovation in the rapidly evolving healthcare landscape. However, challenges such as data privacy, security, and interoperability must be addressed to realize the full potential of Big Data in healthcare.

Big Data has become an indispensable tool in the field of marketing, revolutionizing how companies understand, target, and engage with their customers. In this section, we will explore the role of Big Data in marketing, including its applications, benefits, challenges, and deployment techniques using command-line interface (CLI) commands or specialized tools.

Customer Segmentation: Customer segmentation is the process of dividing a target market into distinct groups based on shared characteristics or behaviors. Big Data enables marketers to segment customers more effectively by analyzing vast amounts of data, including demographics, purchase history, browsing behavior, and social media interactions. CLI commands can be used to perform segmentation analysis using statistical software packages like R or Python.

For example, in R, we can use the k-means clustering algorithm to segment customers based on their purchase behavior:

cssCopy code

```
kmeans_model                                <-
kmeans(customer_data[,c('purchase_frequency',
'average_order_value')], centers=3)
```

This command will perform k-means clustering on the specified variables in the customer data, dividing customers into three segments based on their purchase frequency and average order value.

Personalized Marketing: Personalized marketing involves tailoring marketing messages and offers to individual customers based on their preferences, behaviors, and past interactions with the brand. Big Data enables marketers to deliver personalized experiences at scale by analyzing customer data and leveraging machine learning algorithms to predict customer preferences. CLI commands can be used to train predictive models and generate personalized recommendations.

For example, in Python, we can use the scikit-learn library to train a collaborative filtering model for personalized recommendations:

javaCopy code

```
from sklearn.neighbors import NearestNeighbors
model = NearestNeighbors(n_neighbors=5, algorithm='brute', metric='cosine')
model.fit(customer_purchase_history)
```

This command will train a nearest neighbors model on the customer purchase history data, allowing marketers to generate personalized product recommendations for individual customers.

Marketing Attribution: Marketing attribution is the process of determining the impact of marketing channels and campaigns on customer behavior and conversion outcomes. Big Data enables marketers to track and analyze customer touchpoints across multiple channels, including email, social media, search, and offline interactions. CLI commands can be used to analyze attribution data and calculate the contribution of each marketing channel to conversions.

For example, in SQL, we can use window functions to perform time-series analysis and calculate attribution metrics:

sqlCopy code

```sql
SELECT channel, SUM(revenue) OVER (PARTITION BY channel ORDER BY date ROWS BETWEEN UNBOUNDED PRECEDING AND CURRENT ROW) AS cumulative_revenue FROM attribution_data;
```

This command will calculate the cumulative revenue generated by each marketing channel over time, allowing marketers to assess the effectiveness of their campaigns.

Predictive Modeling: Predictive modeling involves using historical data to make predictions about future outcomes or behaviors. In marketing, predictive modeling can be used to forecast customer lifetime value, churn risk, purchase propensity, and other key metrics. CLI commands can be used to train predictive models and generate insights that inform marketing strategy and decision-making.

For example, in R, we can use the caret package to train a predictive model for customer churn prediction:

scssCopy code

```scss
library(caret) model <- train(churn ~ ., data=customer_data, method='glm')
```

This command will train a logistic regression model to predict customer churn based on various features in the customer data.

In summary, Big Data has transformed the field of marketing, enabling marketers to gain deeper insights into customer behavior, personalize marketing efforts, and optimize campaign performance. By leveraging CLI commands and specialized analytics tools, marketers can harness the power of Big Data to drive growth, increase customer engagement, and achieve competitive advantage in today's data-driven marketing landscape. However, challenges such as data privacy, integration, and interpretation must be addressed to fully realize the potential of Big Data in marketing.

BOOK 2
DATA MINING TECHNIQUES
EXPLORING PATTERNS AND INSIGHTS IN BIG DATA

ROB BOTWRIGHT

Chapter 1: Introduction to Data Mining

Data mining, also known as knowledge discovery in databases (KDD), has a rich history and has evolved significantly over the years, driven by advancements in technology, computing power, and the increasing availability of data. In this section, we will explore the historical milestones and key developments in the field of data mining, tracing its evolution from its early beginnings to its current state, and discuss the deployment techniques using command-line interface (CLI) commands or specialized tools.

Early Beginnings: The roots of data mining can be traced back to the 1960s and 1970s, when researchers began exploring methods for automated pattern recognition and information retrieval. One of the earliest data mining techniques was the Apriori algorithm, developed by Agrawal et al. in 1994, for association rule mining in large transaction databases. The Apriori algorithm laid the foundation for future developments in data mining and paved the way for the emergence of more sophisticated techniques.

CLI command to deploy Apriori algorithm in R:

```
scssCopy code
library(arules)                transactions        <-
read.transactions('transaction_data.csv',
format='single')    rules    <-    apriori(transactions,
parameter=list(support=0.1, confidence=0.5))
```

This command will read transaction data from a CSV file, apply the Apriori algorithm to mine association rules, and generate a set of rules based on the specified support and confidence thresholds.

Growth and Expansion: In the 1990s and early 2000s, data mining gained momentum as organizations began to recognize its potential for extracting valuable insights from large datasets. During this period, a variety of data mining techniques and algorithms were developed, including decision trees, neural networks, and clustering algorithms. These techniques enabled analysts to uncover hidden patterns, relationships, and trends in data, leading to improvements in business operations, marketing strategies, and decision-making processes.

CLI command to deploy decision tree algorithm in Python with scikit-learn:

scssCopy code

```
from sklearn.tree import DecisionTreeClassifier model
= DecisionTreeClassifier() model.fit(X_train, y_train)
```

This command will train a decision tree classifier model using the training data and the scikit-learn library in Python.

Emergence of Big Data: The advent of Big Data in the late 2000s brought about a paradigm shift in data mining, as organizations began grappling with increasingly large and complex datasets. Traditional data mining techniques struggled to cope with the scale and variety of data generated by social media, sensors, and other sources. As a result, new approaches and tools for scalable data mining and machine learning were developed, including MapReduce, Hadoop, and Spark.

CLI command to deploy MapReduce for data mining:
luaCopy code

```
mapreduce.jar -input input_data.txt -output output_directory -mapper mapper.py -reducer reducer.py
```

This command will run a MapReduce job to process and analyze input data using the mapper and reducer scripts.

Integration of Machine Learning: In recent years, data mining has become increasingly intertwined with machine learning, as organizations seek to leverage advanced algorithms and techniques for predictive modeling, classification, and clustering. Machine learning algorithms such as random forests, support vector machines, and deep learning have become indispensable tools for data mining practitioners, enabling them to tackle complex problems and extract actionable insights from data.

CLI command to deploy random forest algorithm in R with caret package:
scssCopy code

```
library(caret) model <- train(target_variable ~ ., data=train_data, method='rf')
```

This command will train a random forest model using the caret package in R, with the target variable specified as the outcome variable.

In summary, the history and evolution of data mining reflect a journey of innovation, experimentation, and discovery, driven by the quest to unlock the hidden potential of data. From its humble beginnings in the 1960s to its current state in the era of Big Data and machine learning, data mining has transformed the way organizations analyze data, make decisions, and create value. By embracing CLI commands and leveraging specialized tools and techniques, data mining practitioners can continue to push the boundaries of what is possible, unlocking new insights and opportunities in the ever-expanding landscape of data.

Data mining is a complex and multifaceted field that encompasses a wide range of techniques, algorithms, and methodologies for extracting valuable insights from large datasets. In this section, we will explore some of the key concepts and terminology in data mining, shedding light on the fundamental principles and techniques that underpin the practice of extracting knowledge from data. Throughout our discussion, we will deploy CLI commands or explain how to deploy the techniques to illustrate the practical application of these concepts.

Data Preprocessing: Data preprocessing is a crucial step in data mining that involves cleaning, transforming, and preparing raw data for analysis. It includes tasks such as handling missing values, removing outliers, and standardizing or normalizing data. CLI commands can be used to perform data preprocessing tasks using specialized tools or libraries such as Pandas in Python.

CLI command to handle missing values in a dataset using Pandas:

kotlinCopy code

```
import pandas as pd data = pd.read_csv('dataset.csv')
data.dropna(inplace=True)
```

This command will read a dataset from a CSV file into a Pandas DataFrame and remove rows with missing values.

Feature Selection: Feature selection is the process of selecting a subset of relevant features or variables from a larger set of input variables for use in model building or analysis. It helps reduce dimensionality, improve model performance, and alleviate issues such as overfitting. CLI commands can be used to perform feature selection using techniques such as recursive feature elimination (RFE) or feature importance ranking.

CLI command to perform feature selection using RFE in Python with scikit-learn:

scssCopy code

```
from sklearn.feature_selection import RFE from
sklearn.linear_model import LogisticRegression model
= LogisticRegression() rfe = RFE(model,
n_features_to_select=5) rfe.fit(X, y)
```

This command will fit a logistic regression model to the data and select the top 5 features using recursive feature elimination.

Association Rules: Association rules are a fundamental concept in data mining that capture relationships or associations between items in a dataset. They are commonly used in market basket analysis to identify patterns of co-occurrence among items in transactional data. CLI commands can be used to mine association rules using algorithms such as Apriori or FP-growth.

CLI command to mine association rules using the Apriori algorithm in R with the arules package:

scssCopy code

```
library(arules) transactions <- read.transactions('transaction_data.csv', format='basket') rules <- apriori(transactions, parameter=list(support=0.1, confidence=0.5))
```

This command will read transaction data from a CSV file into a transaction object and mine association rules using the Apriori algorithm.

Clustering: Clustering is a data mining technique that involves grouping similar objects or data points together based on their characteristics or features. It is used for exploratory data analysis, pattern recognition, and anomaly detection. CLI commands can be used to perform clustering using algorithms such as k-means or hierarchical clustering.

CLI command to perform k-means clustering in Python with scikit-learn:

scssCopy code

```
from sklearn.cluster import KMeans kmeans = KMeans(n_clusters=3) kmeans.fit(X)
```

This command will fit a k-means clustering model to the data and assign each data point to one of three clusters.

Classification: Classification is a supervised learning technique in data mining that involves predicting the class or category of a new observation based on its features or attributes. It is used for tasks such as spam detection, sentiment analysis, and disease diagnosis. CLI commands can be used to train classification models using algorithms such as decision trees, logistic regression, or support vector machines.

CLI command to train a decision tree classifier in R with the rpart package:

scssCopy code

```
library(rpart) model <- rpart(target_variable ~ ., data=train_data)
```

This command will train a decision tree classifier using the rpart package in R, with the target variable specified as the outcome variable.

In summary, understanding key concepts and terminology in data mining is essential for practitioners to effectively navigate and utilize the myriad techniques and algorithms available. By deploying CLI commands or specialized tools, practitioners can apply these concepts in practice to extract valuable insights from data, solve real-world problems, and drive business innovation and success.

Chapter 2: Understanding Data Patterns

Identifying patterns in data is a fundamental task in data mining and analysis, enabling organizations to uncover hidden insights, trends, and relationships that can inform decision-making and drive business success. In this section, we will explore various techniques and methodologies for identifying patterns in data, including CLI commands or explanations of how to deploy the techniques to illustrate their practical application.

Exploratory Data Analysis (EDA): Exploratory Data Analysis (EDA) is an essential first step in identifying patterns in data, involving the visualization and summary of data to gain insights into its structure, distribution, and relationships between variables. EDA techniques such as histograms, scatter plots, and correlation matrices can be used to identify patterns visually and explore potential relationships between variables.

CLI command to generate a histogram of a variable in R using the ggplot2 package:

```scss
scssCopy code
library(ggplot2) ggplot(data, aes(x=variable)) + geom_histogram()
```

This command will create a histogram of the specified variable in the dataset using the ggplot2 package in R.

Clustering: Clustering is a technique used to identify groups or clusters of similar objects or data points based on their characteristics or features. It is commonly used in unsupervised learning and can help uncover hidden patterns or structures within the data. Algorithms such as k-means clustering or hierarchical clustering can be deployed to partition the data into clusters based on similarity.

CLI command to perform k-means clustering in Python using scikit-learn:

scssCopy code

```
from sklearn.cluster import KMeans kmeans = KMeans(n_clusters=3) kmeans.fit(data)
```

This command will apply the k-means clustering algorithm to the data and partition it into three clusters based on similarity.

Association Rule Mining: Association rule mining is a technique used to discover interesting relationships or associations between variables in large datasets. It is commonly used in market basket analysis to identify patterns of co-occurrence among items in transactional data. Algorithms such as Apriori or FP-growth can be deployed to mine association rules from the data.

CLI command to mine association rules using the Apriori algorithm in Python with the mlxtend package:

pythonCopy code

```
from mlxtend.frequent_patterns import apriori, association_rules frequent_itemsets = apriori(data, min_support=0.05, use_colnames=True) rules = association_rules(frequent_itemsets, metric='lift', min_threshold=1)
```

This command will mine frequent itemsets using the Apriori algorithm and generate association rules based on the specified minimum support and lift threshold.

Time Series Analysis: Time series analysis is a technique used to identify patterns or trends in sequential data over time. It is commonly used in forecasting, anomaly detection, and trend analysis. Techniques such as autocorrelation plots, moving averages, and exponential smoothing can be deployed to analyze time series data and identify patterns.

CLI command to plot an autocorrelation plot of a time series in Python using the statsmodels library:

kotlinCopy code

```
import                statsmodels.api              as              sm
sm.graphics.tsa.plot_acf(data)
```

This command will generate an autocorrelation plot of the time series data using the statsmodels library in Python.

Text Mining: Text mining is a technique used to extract patterns, insights, and knowledge from unstructured text data. It involves tasks such as text classification, sentiment analysis, and topic modeling. Techniques such as natural language processing (NLP), term frequency-inverse document frequency (TF-IDF), and latent Dirichlet allocation (LDA) can be deployed to analyze text data and identify patterns.

CLI command to perform sentiment analysis on text data in R using the textblob package:

scssCopy code

```
library(textblob)              sentiment                  <-
textblob_sentiment(text_data)
```

This command will analyze the sentiment of the text data using the textblob package in R.

In summary, identifying patterns in data is a critical task in data mining and analysis, enabling organizations to extract valuable insights and make informed decisions. By deploying various techniques such as exploratory data analysis, clustering, association rule mining, time series analysis, and text mining, practitioners can uncover hidden patterns, trends, and relationships within the data, driving innovation and creating value for businesses and society.

In the realm of data analysis, distinguishing between patterns and noise is essential for deriving meaningful insights and making informed decisions. Patterns represent underlying structures, trends, or relationships within the data, while noise refers to random variation or irrelevant information that obscures the underlying patterns. In this section, we will delve into the concepts of patterns and noise, explore techniques for discriminating between them, and discuss strategies for interpreting and making sense of the identified patterns. Throughout our discussion, we will deploy CLI commands or provide explanations on how to deploy the techniques to illustrate their practical application.

Data Visualization: Data visualization is a powerful tool for discriminating between patterns and noise by visually exploring the data and identifying meaningful structures or trends. Techniques such as scatter plots, line charts, and heatmaps can help reveal patterns, while anomalies or random fluctuations may appear as outliers or irregularities in the visualization. By visually inspecting the data, analysts can gain insights into its underlying structure and distinguish between meaningful patterns and noise.

CLI command to generate a scatter plot of two variables in Python using matplotlib:

kotlinCopy code

```
import matplotlib.pyplot as plt
plt.scatter(data['variable1'], data['variable2'])
plt.xlabel('Variable 1') plt.ylabel('Variable 2')
plt.title('Scatter Plot of Variable 1 vs. Variable 2')
plt.show()
```

This command will generate a scatter plot of two variables from the dataset using the matplotlib library in Python, allowing analysts to visually assess the relationship between the variables and identify any discernible patterns or outliers.

Statistical Analysis: Statistical analysis provides a rigorous framework for discriminating between patterns and noise by quantifying the degree of association or significance between variables. Techniques such as correlation analysis, hypothesis testing, and regression analysis can help assess the strength and significance of relationships within the data, distinguishing between meaningful patterns and random fluctuations. By applying statistical tests and measures, analysts can identify patterns that are statistically significant and worthy of further investigation.

CLI command to perform correlation analysis in R using the corrplot package:

scssCopy code

```
library(corrplot) correlation_matrix <- cor(data)
corrplot(correlation_matrix, method='pearson')
```

This command will compute the correlation matrix for the variables in the dataset and visualize the correlations using a correlation plot, allowing analysts to identify strong correlations indicative of underlying patterns.

Machine Learning: Machine learning algorithms offer a powerful approach to discriminating between patterns and noise by automatically identifying complex patterns or relationships within the data. Techniques such as supervised learning, unsupervised learning, and anomaly detection can help uncover meaningful patterns while filtering out noise or irrelevant information. By training machine learning models on labeled data or clustering algorithms on unlabeled data, analysts can identify patterns that generalize well to new data, distinguishing them from random fluctuations or noise.

CLI command to train a decision tree classifier in Python using scikit-learn:

scssCopy code

```
from sklearn.tree import DecisionTreeClassifier from sklearn.model_selection import train_test_split X_train, X_test, y_train, y_test = train_test_split(X, y, test_size=0.2, random_state=42) model = DecisionTreeClassifier() model.fit(X_train, y_train)
```

This command will split the data into training and testing sets, train a decision tree classifier on the training data, and evaluate its performance on the testing data, allowing analysts to assess the model's ability to discriminate between patterns and noise.

Domain Knowledge and Context: Domain knowledge and context play a crucial role in interpreting patterns and distinguishing them from noise by providing insights into the underlying processes or phenomena being observed. By leveraging domain expertise and contextual information, analysts can validate identified patterns, assess their relevance, and interpret their implications in the context of the problem domain. Domain knowledge can help identify spurious correlations, confounding factors, or other sources of noise that may obscure the underlying patterns in the data.

In summary, discriminating between patterns and noise is a fundamental task in data analysis, requiring a combination of visualization techniques, statistical analysis, machine learning algorithms, and domain expertise. By deploying CLI commands or specialized tools and applying a rigorous analytical approach, analysts can uncover meaningful patterns within the data, filter out irrelevant noise, and derive actionable insights that drive decision-making and innovation.

Chapter 3: Data Preprocessing for Mining

Data cleaning, also known as data cleansing or data scrubbing, is a critical step in the data preparation process that involves identifying and correcting errors, inconsistencies, and missing values in the dataset. Clean data is essential for ensuring the accuracy, reliability, and integrity of analytical results and insights derived from the data. In this section, we will explore various data cleaning techniques, including CLI commands or explanations of how to deploy the techniques to illustrate their practical application.

Handling Missing Values: Missing values are a common issue in real-world datasets and can arise due to various reasons such as data entry errors, equipment malfunction, or incomplete records. Handling missing values is a crucial aspect of data cleaning, and there are several techniques for dealing with them, including imputation, deletion, or interpolation.

CLI command to handle missing values in Python using the pandas library:

pythonCopy code

```
import pandas as pd # Read the dataset into a pandas DataFrame  data = pd.read_csv('dataset.csv') # Replace missing values with the mean of the column data.fillna(data.mean(), inplace=True)
```

This command will read the dataset from a CSV file into a pandas DataFrame and replace missing values with the mean of the column using the fillna() function.

Removing Duplicates: Duplicate records can skew analytical results and introduce bias into the analysis. Removing duplicates is an essential data cleaning technique to ensure the accuracy and integrity of the dataset. Duplicate records can be identified based on one or more key columns, and duplicate rows can be removed to retain only unique records.

CLI command to remove duplicate rows in SQL using the DISTINCT keyword:

sqlCopy code

```sql
SELECT DISTINCT * FROM table_name;
```

This command will select only distinct rows from the specified table, removing duplicate records based on all columns.

Standardizing Data: Standardizing data involves converting data into a consistent format or representation to facilitate analysis and comparison. It often involves converting categorical variables into numerical representations, scaling numerical variables to a common range, or normalizing data to have a mean of zero and a standard deviation of one.

CLI command to standardize data in Python using the scikit-learn library:

scssCopy code

```
from sklearn.preprocessing import StandardScaler
scaler = StandardScaler() scaled_data =
scaler.fit_transform(data)
```

This command will scale the numerical variables in the dataset to have a mean of zero and a standard deviation of one using the StandardScaler() class.

Handling Outliers: Outliers are data points that deviate significantly from the rest of the data and can distort statistical analyses and machine learning models. Handling outliers is essential for ensuring the robustness and reliability of analytical results. Techniques for handling outliers include trimming, winsorization, or transforming the data using robust statistical measures.

CLI command to detect and remove outliers in Python using the scipy library:

pythonCopy code

```
from scipy import stats # Calculate z-scores for each
data point z_scores = stats.zscore(data) # Filter out
data points with z-scores above a threshold
filtered_data = data[(z_scores < 3).all(axis=1)]
```

This command will calculate z-scores for each data point and filter out data points with z-scores above a threshold of three standard deviations from the mean.

Data Validation: Data validation involves checking the integrity and accuracy of the data to ensure that it meets predefined quality standards or criteria. Techniques for data validation include range checks, format checks, and consistency checks to identify errors or anomalies in the data.

CLI command to perform data validation in Python using the pandas library:

sqlCopy code

```
# Perform range check on a numerical variable
data['numerical_column'].between(0, 100, inclusive=True).all()
```

This command will perform a range check on the specified numerical column to ensure that all values fall within the specified range.

In summary, data cleaning is a critical step in the data preparation process that involves identifying and correcting errors, inconsistencies, and missing values in the dataset. By deploying various data cleaning techniques such as handling missing values, removing duplicates, standardizing data, handling outliers, and performing data validation, analysts can ensure the accuracy, reliability, and integrity of the data, leading to more robust analytical results and insights.

Data transformation is a crucial preprocessing step in data analysis and machine learning, involving the conversion of raw data into a format that is more suitable for analysis or modeling. In this section, we will explore various data transformation methods, including CLI commands or explanations of how to deploy the techniques to illustrate their practical application.

Scaling and Normalization: Scaling and normalization are techniques used to standardize the scale or range of numerical variables in the dataset, making them comparable and reducing the influence of variables with larger scales on the analysis. Scaling involves transforming numerical variables to a common scale, while normalization involves rescaling variables to have a specific distribution or range, such as a mean of zero and a standard deviation of one.

CLI command to perform scaling and normalization in Python using the scikit-learn library:

makefileCopy code

```
from sklearn.preprocessing import StandardScaler,
MinMaxScaler # Standardize numerical variables using
StandardScaler scaler = StandardScaler() scaled_data
= scaler.fit_transform(data) # Normalize numerical
variables using MinMaxScaler minmax_scaler =
MinMaxScaler()          normalized_data          =
minmax_scaler.fit_transform(data)
```

This command will scale numerical variables to have a mean of zero and a standard deviation of one using StandardScaler, and normalize numerical variables to the range [0, 1] using MinMaxScaler.

Log Transformation: Log transformation is a technique used to stabilize the variance and make the distribution of numerical variables more symmetrical. It is particularly useful for variables with highly skewed distributions or variables with a wide range of values. Log transformation involves taking the logarithm of the variable values, typically using the natural logarithm or base-10 logarithm.

CLI command to perform log transformation in Python using the numpy library:

pythonCopy code

```
import numpy as np # Log transform a numerical variable using numpy log_transformed_data = np.log(data['numerical_variable'] + 1)
```

This command will perform a log transformation on the specified numerical variable, adding one to handle zero values before taking the logarithm.

Box-Cox Transformation: The Box-Cox transformation is a more flexible alternative to log transformation that can handle both positively and negatively skewed data. It is used to stabilize variance and make the distribution of numerical variables more Gaussian-like. The Box-Cox transformation involves applying a power transformation to the data, with the power parameter lambda determined empirically to achieve the best transformation.

CLI command to perform Box-Cox transformation in Python using the scipy library:

pythonCopy code

```
from scipy.stats import boxcox # Perform Box-Cox transformation on a numerical variable transformed_data, lambda_value = boxcox(data['numerical_variable'])
```

This command will perform Box-Cox transformation on the specified numerical variable and return the transformed data along with the optimal lambda value.

Dummy Coding: Dummy coding, also known as one-hot encoding, is a technique used to convert categorical variables into numerical representations that can be used in mathematical models or analyses. It involves creating binary indicator variables for each category of the categorical variable, where a value of one indicates the presence of the category and zero indicates absence.

CLI command to perform dummy coding in Python using the pandas library:

cssCopy code

```
# Perform one-hot encoding on a categorical variable
encoded_data = pd.get_dummies(data, columns=['categorical_variable'])
```

This command will perform one-hot encoding on the specified categorical variable, creating binary indicator variables for each category.

In summary, data transformation is a critical preprocessing step that involves converting raw data into a format that is more suitable for analysis or modeling. By deploying various data transformation techniques such as scaling and normalization, log transformation, Box-Cox transformation, and dummy coding, analysts can preprocess the data effectively and prepare it for further analysis or modeling. These techniques help improve the accuracy and performance of analytical models and ensure that insights derived from the data are robust and reliable.

Chapter 4: Association Rule Mining

The Apriori algorithm is a fundamental technique in data mining and association rule learning, used to discover frequent itemsets in transactional datasets and derive association rules between items. In this section, we will delve into the principle behind the Apriori algorithm, explore its implementation, and discuss its practical application using CLI commands or explanations on how to deploy the technique.

The principle behind the Apriori algorithm is rooted in the concept of "apriori" property, which states that any subset of a frequent itemset must also be frequent. This property enables efficient pruning of the search space and reduces the computational complexity of discovering frequent itemsets.

Generating Candidate Itemsets: The first step in the Apriori algorithm is to generate candidate itemsets of size k, where k is the length of the itemsets being considered. Candidate itemsets are generated by combining frequent itemsets of size k-1. If all subsets of a candidate itemset are frequent, then the candidate itemset is also considered frequent.

CLI command to generate candidate itemsets of size k in Python using the mlxtend library:

pythonCopy code

```
from mlxtend.frequent_patterns import apriori #
Generate frequent itemsets with minimum support
threshold frequent_itemsets = apriori(data,
```

min_support=0.1, use_colnames=True) # Generate candidate itemsets of size k+1 candidate_itemsets = apriori(data, min_support=0.1, use_colnames=True, max_len=k+1)

This command will generate frequent itemsets from the dataset using the Apriori algorithm with a specified minimum support threshold and then generate candidate itemsets of size k+1.

Pruning Infrequent Itemsets: After generating candidate itemsets, the next step is to prune infrequent itemsets that do not meet the minimum support threshold. Infrequent itemsets are unlikely to be part of any association rule and can be discarded to reduce the search space.

CLI command to prune infrequent itemsets in Python using the mlxtend library:

pythonCopy code

```
from mlxtend.frequent_patterns import association_rules # Generate association rules from frequent itemsets rules = association_rules(frequent_itemsets, metric='confidence', min_threshold=0.5)
```

This command will generate association rules from frequent itemsets using the mlxtend library in Python, specifying a minimum confidence threshold of 0.5.

Mining Association Rules: Once frequent itemsets have been identified, the Apriori algorithm mines association rules by calculating measures such as support, confidence, and lift for each rule. Association rules with sufficiently high support, confidence, and lift are considered interesting and can be used for decision-making or recommendation purposes.

CLI command to mine association rules in Python using the mlxtend library:

pythonCopy code

```
from mlxtend.frequent_patterns import association_rules # Generate association rules from frequent itemsets rules = association_rules(frequent_itemsets, metric='confidence', min_threshold=0.5)
```

This command will generate association rules from frequent itemsets using the mlxtend library in Python, specifying a minimum confidence threshold of 0.5.

Interpretation and Application: Once association rules have been mined, they can be interpreted and applied to real-world problems or datasets. Association rules provide insights into the relationships between items in transactional datasets and can be used for various applications such as market basket analysis, cross-selling, or recommendation systems.

CLI command to interpret association rules in Python using the mlxtend library:

bashCopy code

```
# Print the generated association rules print(rules)
```

This command will print the generated association rules, including antecedent, consequent, support, confidence, and lift, allowing analysts to interpret the rules and derive insights from them.

In summary, the Apriori algorithm is a powerful technique for discovering frequent itemsets and mining association rules in transactional datasets. By leveraging the apriori property and efficient pruning techniques, the Apriori algorithm can efficiently explore the search space and identify meaningful patterns in the data. Through its implementation and interpretation, the Apriori algorithm enables analysts to derive actionable insights and make informed decisions in various domains and applications.

The FP-Growth algorithm is a powerful technique in data mining and frequent pattern mining, designed to efficiently discover frequent itemsets in transactional datasets without the need to generate candidate itemsets explicitly. In this section, we will explore the advantages of the FP-Growth algorithm, its implementation, and practical applications, using CLI commands or explanations on how to deploy the technique.

Advantages of FP-Growth Algorithm: The FP-Growth algorithm offers several advantages over traditional frequent pattern mining algorithms such as Apriori. One of the key advantages is its efficiency in handling large and sparse datasets. Unlike Apriori, which generates candidate itemsets explicitly, FP-Growth constructs a compact data structure called the FP-tree, which represents the dataset in a compressed form. This allows FP-Growth to perform frequent pattern mining with significantly reduced memory and computational overhead.

CLI command to run FP-Growth algorithm in Python using the mlxtend library:

pythonCopy code

```
from mlxtend.frequent_patterns import fpgrowth # Generate frequent itemsets using FP-Growth algorithm frequent_itemsets = fpgrowth(data, min_support=0.1, use_colnames=True)
```

This command will generate frequent itemsets from the dataset using the FP-Growth algorithm with a specified minimum support threshold.

Scalability: Another advantage of the FP-Growth algorithm is its scalability to large datasets. By constructing the FP-tree and using a depth-first traversal approach, FP-Growth can efficiently mine frequent itemsets from massive transactional datasets with millions of transactions and thousands of items. This makes FP-Growth suitable for applications in domains with large-scale transactional data, such as retail, e-commerce, and web log analysis.

CLI command to deploy FP-Growth algorithm on large datasets in Python using the Dask library:

pythonCopy code

```
import dask.dataframe as dd from mlxtend.frequent_patterns import fpgrowth # Load data as Dask DataFrame for parallel processing data = dd.read_csv('large_dataset.csv') # Generate frequent itemsets using FP-Growth algorithm frequent_itemsets = fpgrowth(data, min_support=0.1, use_colnames=True)
```

This command will load the large dataset as a Dask DataFrame for parallel processing and then generate frequent itemsets using the FP-Growth algorithm.

Handling Sparse Data: FP-Growth is particularly well-suited for handling sparse datasets where most itemsets occur infrequently. The FP-tree data structure efficiently captures the frequent patterns in the dataset while eliminating the need to store and manipulate the entire transaction database explicitly. This enables FP-Growth to handle sparse datasets more effectively than Apriori, which may suffer from performance degradation in such scenarios.

CLI command to deploy FP-Growth algorithm on sparse datasets in Python using the scipy.sparse library:

pythonCopy code

```
from scipy.sparse import csr_matrix from
mlxtend.frequent_patterns import fpgrowth #
Convert sparse dataset to compressed sparse row
(CSR) matrix sparse_data = csr_matrix(data) #
Generate frequent itemsets using FP-Growth
algorithm frequent_itemsets = fpgrowth(sparse_data,
min_support=0.1, use_colnames=True)
```

This command will convert the sparse dataset to a compressed sparse row (CSR) matrix and then generate frequent itemsets using the FP-Growth algorithm.

Practical Applications: The FP-Growth algorithm finds applications in various domains and industries, including market basket analysis, recommendation systems, customer segmentation, and fraud detection. By discovering frequent itemsets and association rules from transactional datasets, FP-Growth enables organizations to uncover hidden patterns, understand customer behavior, and make data-driven decisions.

CLI command to apply FP-Growth algorithm for market basket analysis in Python using the mlxtend library:

pythonCopy code

```
from mlxtend.frequent_patterns import association_rules # Generate association rules from frequent itemsets using FP-Growth algorithm rules = association_rules(frequent_itemsets, metric='confidence', min_threshold=0.5)
```

This command will generate association rules from frequent itemsets using the FP-Growth algorithm and filter the rules based on a specified confidence threshold, allowing analysts to derive actionable insights for market basket analysis.

In summary, the FP-Growth algorithm offers several advantages over traditional frequent pattern mining algorithms, including efficiency, scalability, and effectiveness in handling sparse data. Through its implementation and practical applications, FP-Growth enables organizations to extract valuable insights from transactional datasets, drive business growth, and gain a competitive edge in the marketplace.

Chapter 5: Classification Techniques

Decision trees are a versatile and widely used machine learning algorithm that can perform both classification and regression tasks. In this section, we will explore the construction and evaluation of decision trees, discussing their principles, implementation, and practical applications using CLI commands or explanations on how to deploy the technique.

Construction of Decision Trees: The construction of a decision tree involves recursively partitioning the input space into regions based on the values of input features, such that each region is as homogeneous as possible with respect to the target variable. This process is guided by selecting the best split at each node of the tree based on a specific criterion, such as Gini impurity for classification or mean squared error for regression.

CLI command to construct a decision tree for classification in Python using the scikit-learn library:

pythonCopy code

```
from sklearn.tree import DecisionTreeClassifier # Initialize decision tree classifier clf = DecisionTreeClassifier() # Fit the classifier to the training data clf.fit(X_train, y_train)
```

This command will initialize a decision tree classifier and fit it to the training data, where X_train represents the input features and y_train represents the target variable.

Evaluation of Decision Trees: The evaluation of a decision tree involves assessing its performance on unseen data to measure its predictive accuracy and generalization ability. Common evaluation metrics for classification tasks include accuracy, precision, recall, F1-score, and area under the receiver operating characteristic curve (ROC AUC). For regression tasks, evaluation metrics may include mean absolute error, mean squared error, and R-squared.

CLI command to evaluate a decision tree classifier in Python using the scikit-learn library:

pythonCopy code

```
from sklearn.metrics import accuracy_score # Predict the target variable on the test data y_pred = clf.predict(X_test) # Calculate accuracy of the classifier accuracy = accuracy_score(y_test, y_pred) print("Accuracy:", accuracy)
```

This command will predict the target variable on the test data using the trained decision tree classifier and calculate the accuracy of the classifier.

Overfitting and Pruning: One of the challenges in building decision trees is overfitting, where the tree captures noise or irrelevant patterns in the training data, leading to poor generalization on unseen data. To mitigate overfitting, various pruning techniques can be applied, such as setting a maximum depth for the tree, imposing minimum samples per leaf or split, or using ensemble methods like Random Forest or Gradient Boosting.

CLI command to control the depth of a decision tree classifier in Python using the scikit-learn library:

pythonCopy code

```python
# Initialize decision tree classifier with maximum depth
clf = DecisionTreeClassifier(max_depth=5) # Fit the
classifier to the training data clf.fit(X_train, y_train)
```

This command will initialize a decision tree classifier with a maximum depth of five levels and fit it to the training data, controlling the complexity of the tree.

Feature Importance: Decision trees provide a natural way to assess the importance of input features in predicting the target variable. Feature importance scores can be calculated based on the impurity reduction or information gain achieved by each feature during the construction of the tree. This information can be valuable for feature selection and understanding the underlying data patterns.

CLI command to compute feature importance of a decision tree classifier in Python using the scikit-learn library:

pythonCopy code

```python
# Retrieve feature importance scores from the trained
classifier                   feature_importance           =
clf.feature_importances_ # Print feature importance
scores            print("Feature            Importance:",
feature_importance)
```

This command will retrieve the feature importance scores from the trained decision tree classifier, providing insights into the relative importance of each input feature.

Practical Applications: Decision trees find applications in various domains, including finance, healthcare, marketing, and customer relationship management. They are used for tasks such as credit scoring, disease diagnosis, churn prediction, and product recommendation. Decision trees are particularly well-suited for scenarios where interpretability, ease of use, and explainability are important considerations.

CLI command to apply decision tree classifier for credit scoring in Python using the scikit-learn library:

pythonCopy code

```
# Initialize decision tree classifier clf = DecisionTreeClassifier() # Fit the classifier to the training data clf.fit(X_train, y_train) # Predict credit scores on new applicants credit_scores = clf.predict(new_applicants_data)
```

This command will initialize a decision tree classifier, fit it to the training data, and use it to predict credit scores for new applicants, enabling financial institutions to assess creditworthiness and make lending decisions.

In summary, decision trees are powerful and interpretable machine learning algorithms that can be effectively used for both classification and regression tasks. By understanding the principles of decision tree construction, evaluating their performance, mitigating overfitting through pruning techniques, assessing feature importance, and applying them to real-world applications, practitioners can harness the full potential of decision trees for solving a wide range of predictive modeling problems.

Support Vector Machines: Theory and Practical Considerations:

Support Vector Machines (SVMs) are powerful supervised learning models used for classification and regression tasks. In this section, we will delve into the theory behind Support Vector Machines, discuss practical considerations for their deployment, and provide insights into their implementation using CLI commands or explanations.

Theory of Support Vector Machines: Support Vector Machines are based on the concept of finding the optimal hyperplane that separates data points belonging to different classes in a high-dimensional space. The hyperplane is chosen to maximize the margin, which is the distance between the hyperplane and the closest data points from each class, known as support vectors. This optimization problem is typically formulated as a convex quadratic programming problem and solved using techniques such as the Sequential Minimal Optimization (SMO) algorithm.

CLI command to train a Support Vector Machine classifier for binary classification in Python using the scikit-learn library:

pythonCopy code

```
from sklearn.svm import SVC # Initialize Support Vector Machine classifier svm_classifier = SVC(kernel='linear', C=1.0) # Fit the classifier to the training data svm_classifier.fit(X_train, y_train)
```

This command will initialize a Support Vector Machine classifier with a linear kernel and regularization parameter C=1.0, and fit it to the training data.

Practical Considerations for SVMs: Support Vector Machines offer several advantages, including their ability to handle high-dimensional data, their effectiveness in dealing with non-linear separable data through kernel tricks, and their robustness to overfitting when appropriate regularization is applied. However, SVMs also have some practical considerations that need to be taken into account, such as the choice of kernel function, the selection of hyperparameters (e.g., regularization parameter C), and their computational complexity, especially for large-scale datasets.

CLI command to train a Support Vector Machine classifier with a non-linear kernel (e.g., radial basis function kernel) in Python using the scikit-learn library:

pythonCopy code

```
# Initialize Support Vector Machine classifier with a non-linear kernel svm_classifier = SVC(kernel='rbf', gamma=0.1, C=1.0) # Fit the classifier to the training data svm_classifier.fit(X_train, y_train)
```

This command will initialize a Support Vector Machine classifier with a radial basis function (RBF) kernel and regularization parameter C=1.0, and fit it to the training data.

Hyperparameter Tuning: Hyperparameter tuning is an essential step in optimizing the performance of Support Vector Machines. The choice of hyperparameters, such as the kernel type, regularization parameter C, and kernel-specific parameters (e.g., gamma for the RBF kernel), can significantly impact the model's performance and generalization ability. Techniques such as cross-validation and grid search can be employed to search for the optimal combination of hyperparameters.

CLI command to perform hyperparameter tuning for a Support Vector Machine classifier using grid search cross-validation in Python using the scikit-learn library:
pythonCopy code

```
from sklearn.model_selection import GridSearchCV # Define the hyperparameter grid param_grid = {'kernel': ['linear', 'rbf'], 'C': [0.1, 1.0, 10.0], 'gamma': [0.01, 0.1, 1.0]} # Initialize Support Vector Machine classifier svm_classifier = SVC() # Perform grid search cross-validation grid_search = GridSearchCV(estimator=svm_classifier, param_grid=param_grid, cv=5) grid_search.fit(X_train, y_train) # Get the best hyperparameters best_params = grid_search.best_params_
```

This command will perform grid search cross-validation to find the best combination of hyperparameters for the Support Vector Machine classifier.

Interpretability and Visualization: One limitation of Support Vector Machines is their lack of interpretability compared to simpler models like decision trees or linear regression. However, some techniques can be employed to interpret SVMs, such as examining the support vectors, visualizing decision boundaries, and analyzing feature importance.

CLI command to visualize decision boundaries of a Support Vector Machine classifier in Python using the matplotlib library:
pythonCopy code

```
import matplotlib.pyplot as plt from mlxtend.plotting import plot_decision_regions # Visualize decision boundaries of the trained classifier
```

```
plot_decision_regions(X_train.values,    y_train.values,
clf=svm_classifier,    legend=2)    plt.xlabel('Feature    1')
plt.ylabel('Feature 2') plt.title('Decision Boundary of
Support Vector Machine Classifier') plt.show()
```

This command will visualize the decision boundaries of
the trained Support Vector Machine classifier, providing
insights into its behavior and discriminative power.

In summary, Support Vector Machines are versatile and
powerful machine learning models that offer robust
performance for classification and regression tasks. By
understanding the theoretical underpinnings of SVMs,
considering   practical   considerations   for   their
deployment, tuning hyperparameters effectively, and
employing   techniques   for   interpretation   and
visualization, practitioners can leverage the full
potential of Support Vector Machines for a wide range
of real-world applications.

Chapter 6: Clustering Analysis

K-Means clustering is one of the most popular unsupervised learning algorithms used for partitioning data into clusters based on similarity. In this section, we will explore the K-Means clustering algorithm, discuss its variants and extensions, and provide insights into their implementation using CLI commands or explanations.

K-Means Clustering Algorithm: The K-Means clustering algorithm is a simple yet effective approach to partitioning a dataset into K clusters. The algorithm works by iteratively assigning data points to the nearest cluster centroid and updating the centroids based on the mean of the data points assigned to each cluster. This process continues until convergence, where the centroids no longer change significantly, or until a predefined number of iterations is reached.

CLI command to perform K-Means clustering in Python using the scikit-learn library:

pythonCopy code

```
from sklearn.cluster import KMeans # Initialize K-Means clustering algorithm with K clusters kmeans = KMeans(n_clusters=3) # Fit the algorithm to the data kmeans.fit(X)
```

This command will initialize a K-Means clustering algorithm with three clusters and fit it to the data represented by the feature matrix X.

Variants of K-Means Clustering: Several variants and extensions of the K-Means clustering algorithm have been proposed to address its limitations and improve its performance in various scenarios.

a. K-Means++: K-Means++ is an extension of the K-Means algorithm that addresses the issue of initialization sensitivity. Instead of randomly initializing cluster centroids, K-Means++ selects initial centroids that are far away from each other, resulting in more stable and accurate clustering.

CLI command to perform K-Means++ clustering in Python using the scikit-learn library:

pythonCopy code

```
from sklearn.cluster import KMeans # Initialize K-Means++ clustering algorithm with K clusters kmeans = KMeans(n_clusters=3, init='k-means++') # Fit the algorithm to the data kmeans.fit(X)
```

This command will initialize a K-Means++ clustering algorithm with three clusters and fit it to the data.

b. Mini-Batch K-Means: Mini-Batch K-Means is a variant of the K-Means algorithm that uses mini-batches of data to update cluster centroids, making it more computationally efficient and scalable to large datasets.

CLI command to perform Mini-Batch K-Means clustering in Python using the scikit-learn library:

pythonCopy code

```
from sklearn.cluster import MiniBatchKMeans # Initialize Mini-Batch K-Means clustering algorithm with K clusters minibatch_kmeans =
```

MiniBatchKMeans(n_clusters=3) # Fit the algorithm to the data minibatch_kmeans.fit(X)

This command will initialize a Mini-Batch K-Means clustering algorithm with three clusters and fit it to the data.

c. Kernel K-Means: Kernel K-Means is a non-linear extension of the K-Means algorithm that applies kernel trick to map data into a higher-dimensional space, where clusters are more separable, allowing for more flexible and expressive clustering.

CLI command to perform Kernel K-Means clustering in Python using the KernelKMeans library:

pythonCopy code

from sklearn.cluster import KernelKMeans # Initialize Kernel K-Means clustering algorithm with K clusters kernel_kmeans = KernelKMeans(n_clusters=3, kernel='rbf') # Fit the algorithm to the data kernel_kmeans.fit(X)

This command will initialize a Kernel K-Means clustering algorithm with three clusters and fit it to the data using a radial basis function (RBF) kernel.

Practical Considerations: When deploying K-Means clustering algorithms, several practical considerations need to be taken into account, such as choosing the appropriate number of clusters (K), selecting the initialization method, handling high-dimensional data, and evaluating clustering performance using metrics such as silhouette score or Davies-Bouldin index.

CLI command to select the optimal number of clusters using the Elbow method in Python:

pythonCopy code

```
import matplotlib.pyplot as plt from sklearn.cluster
import KMeans from yellowbrick.cluster import
KElbowVisualizer # Instantiate the KMeans model
kmeans = KMeans() # Instantiate the KElbowVisualizer
with the number of clusters range visualizer =
KElbowVisualizer(kmeans, k=(2,10)) # Fit the data and
visualize the Elbow method visualizer.fit(X)
visualizer.show()
```

This command will visualize the Elbow method to determine the optimal number of clusters for K-Means clustering based on the distortion score.

In summary, K-Means clustering is a versatile and widely used algorithm for partitioning data into clusters. By understanding its algorithmic principles, exploring its variants and extensions, and considering practical considerations for deployment, practitioners can leverage K-Means clustering to uncover hidden patterns, gain insights, and make data-driven decisions in various domains and applications.

Hierarchical clustering is a versatile and widely used method for grouping objects or data points into a hierarchical structure based on their similarity. In this section, we will delve into the methods and applications of hierarchical clustering, discussing its algorithmic principles, variants, practical considerations, and real-world applications, along with CLI commands or explanations on how to deploy the technique.

Algorithmic Principles of Hierarchical Clustering: Hierarchical clustering builds a hierarchical tree-like structure known as a dendrogram, where each node represents a cluster of data points, and the leaves represent individual data points. The algorithm proceeds by iteratively merging the closest clusters or data points based on a chosen similarity metric until all data points are in a single cluster or until a predefined stopping criterion is met. There are two main approaches to hierarchical clustering: agglomerative and divisive.

CLI command to perform agglomerative hierarchical clustering in Python using the scikit-learn library:

pythonCopy code

from sklearn.cluster import AgglomerativeClustering # Initialize Agglomerative clustering algorithm with the number of clusters agglomerative_clustering = AgglomerativeClustering(n_clusters=3) # Fit the algorithm to the data agglomerative_clustering.fit(X)

This command will initialize an Agglomerative clustering algorithm with three clusters and fit it to the data represented by the feature matrix X.

Variants of Hierarchical Clustering: a. Agglomerative Hierarchical Clustering: Agglomerative hierarchical clustering starts with each data point as a separate cluster and iteratively merges the closest pairs of clusters until a single cluster containing all data points is formed. The merging process is guided by a linkage criterion, such as single linkage, complete linkage, or average linkage, which determines the distance between clusters.

CLI command to perform complete linkage hierarchical clustering in Python using the scipy library:

pythonCopy code

```
from scipy.cluster.hierarchy import linkage, dendrogram # Compute the linkage matrix using complete linkage Z = linkage(X, method='complete') # Plot the dendrogram plt.figure(figsize=(10, 5)) dendrogram(Z) plt.title('Complete Linkage Dendrogram') plt.xlabel('Data Points') plt.ylabel('Distance') plt.show()
```

This command will compute the linkage matrix using complete linkage and plot the dendrogram representing the hierarchical clustering structure.

b. Divisive Hierarchical Clustering: Divisive hierarchical clustering starts with all data points in a single cluster and recursively splits clusters into smaller clusters until each cluster contains a single data point. Unlike agglomerative clustering, divisive clustering requires a divisive criterion to determine the optimal split at each step.

Practical Considerations for Hierarchical Clustering: When deploying hierarchical clustering algorithms, several practical considerations need to be taken into account, such as choosing the appropriate linkage criterion, handling high-dimensional data, dealing with missing values or outliers, and determining the optimal number of clusters or the stopping criterion for the clustering process.

CLI command to visualize dendrogram and determine the optimal number of clusters using the elbow method in Python:

pythonCopy code

```
from scipy.cluster.hierarchy import dendrogram from sklearn.cluster import AgglomerativeClustering # Initialize Agglomerative clustering algorithm with a range of clusters agg_clustering = AgglomerativeClustering() # Fit the algorithm to the data agg_clustering.fit(X) # Plot the dendrogram plt.figure(figsize=(10, 5)) dendrogram(agg_clustering, truncate_mode='level', p=5) plt.title('Dendrogram') plt.xlabel('Data Points') plt.ylabel('Distance') plt.show()
```

This command will visualize the dendrogram and allow practitioners to determine the optimal number of clusters based on the elbow method or visual inspection of the dendrogram.

Real-World Applications of Hierarchical Clustering: Hierarchical clustering finds applications in various domains, including biology, finance, social sciences, and marketing. It is used for tasks such as gene expression analysis, portfolio optimization, community detection in social networks, and customer segmentation. Hierarchical clustering enables the identification of meaningful patterns and structures in data, facilitating decision-making and knowledge discovery.

In summary, hierarchical clustering is a powerful and flexible method for organizing data into hierarchical structures based on similarity. By understanding its algorithmic principles, exploring its variants, considering practical considerations for deployment, and applying it to real-world applications, practitioners can leverage hierarchical clustering to gain insights, discover patterns, and extract valuable information from diverse datasets.

Chapter 7: Anomaly Detection

Anomaly detection, also known as outlier detection, is a critical task in data analysis and machine learning aimed at identifying patterns or instances that deviate significantly from the norm. In this section, we will explore various approaches to anomaly detection, including statistical methods, machine learning techniques, and domain-specific approaches, along with CLI commands or explanations on how to deploy the techniques.

Statistical Methods for Anomaly Detection: Statistical methods for anomaly detection rely on modeling the underlying distribution of the data and identifying instances that fall outside a certain threshold or exhibit unusual patterns.

One common statistical approach is the use of z-scores to detect anomalies in univariate data. The z-score measures the number of standard deviations a data point is away from the mean, and data points with high z-scores are considered anomalies.

CLI command to compute z-scores for anomaly detection in Python using the scipy library:

pythonCopy code

```
from scipy.stats import zscore # Compute z-scores for each feature z_scores = zscore(data)
```

This command will compute the z-scores for each feature in the dataset, allowing practitioners to identify outliers based on their deviation from the mean.

Machine Learning Techniques for Anomaly Detection: Machine learning techniques offer powerful tools for anomaly detection, leveraging algorithms to learn patterns and anomalies from labeled or unlabeled data.

One popular machine learning approach is isolation forest, which constructs an ensemble of decision trees and isolates anomalies by measuring the average path length to reach them. Anomalies are expected to have shorter path lengths compared to normal instances.

CLI command to perform anomaly detection using isolation forest in Python using the scikit-learn library: pythonCopy code

```
from sklearn.ensemble import IsolationForest # Initialize Isolation Forest model isolation_forest = IsolationForest(contamination=0.1) # Fit the model to the data isolation_forest.fit(X)
```

This command will initialize an isolation forest model with a contamination parameter specifying the expected proportion of anomalies in the data and fit it to the feature matrix X.

Domain-Specific Approaches to Anomaly Detection: In addition to statistical and machine learning methods, domain-specific approaches tailored to the characteristics of the data and the application domain can also be effective for anomaly detection.

For example, in network security, anomaly detection techniques may focus on identifying unusual patterns in network traffic, such as unexpected spikes in data volume or unusual communication patterns between hosts.

CLI command to deploy a domain-specific anomaly detection technique for network traffic analysis:

bashCopy code

```
# Snort is a popular network intrusion detection system (NIDS) that can be used for anomaly detection
snort -i eth0 -c /etc/snort/snort.conf -l /var/log/snort
```

This command will run Snort on the network interface eth0 using the configuration file snort.conf and log anomalous network activity to the directory /var/log/snort.

Ensemble Methods for Anomaly Detection: Ensemble methods combine multiple anomaly detection techniques to improve overall detection performance and robustness.

For example, an ensemble of isolation forests, k-nearest neighbors, and one-class SVMs can be combined to leverage the strengths of each individual method and achieve better generalization across different types of anomalies.

CLI command to implement an ensemble of anomaly detection methods in Python using the PyOD library:

pythonCopy code

```
from pyod.models.combination import aom, moa, average # Initialize individual anomaly detection models model1 = IsolationForest() model2 = KNN()
```

model3 = OneClassSVM() # Fit individual models to the data model1.fit(X) model2.fit(X) model3.fit(X) # Combine models using average ensemble method ensemble = average([model1.decision_scores_, model2.decision_scores_, model3.decision_scores_])

This command will initialize individual anomaly detection models, fit them to the data, and combine their decision scores using the average ensemble method.

In summary, anomaly detection is a crucial task in data analysis and machine learning, with various approaches available for identifying outliers and unusual patterns in data. By understanding and deploying statistical methods, machine learning techniques, domain-specific approaches, and ensemble methods, practitioners can effectively detect anomalies and mitigate potential risks or abnormalities in diverse datasets and application domains.

Anomaly detection is a critical task in data analysis and machine learning, aimed at identifying instances or patterns that deviate significantly from the norm. In this section, we will explore two main approaches to anomaly detection: supervised and unsupervised techniques. We will discuss their algorithmic principles, advantages, limitations, and real-world applications, along with CLI commands or explanations on how to deploy the techniques.

Supervised Anomaly Detection Techniques: Supervised anomaly detection techniques require labeled data, where anomalies are explicitly identified or labeled by domain experts. These techniques learn from both normal and anomalous instances to build a predictive model that can classify new instances as either normal or anomalous.

One common supervised approach is using classification algorithms, such as support vector machines (SVMs), decision trees, or neural networks, to discriminate between normal and anomalous instances based on their features.

CLI command to train a supervised anomaly detection model using a support vector machine (SVM) in Python using the scikit-learn library:

pythonCopy code

```
from sklearn.svm import OneClassSVM # Initialize One-Class SVM model svm_model = OneClassSVM() # Fit the model to the labeled data svm_model.fit(X_train, y_train)
```

This command will initialize a One-Class SVM model and fit it to the labeled training data represented by the feature matrix X_train and the corresponding labels y_train.

Advantages of supervised anomaly detection techniques include the ability to leverage labeled data for training, which can lead to higher detection accuracy and the ability to distinguish between different types of anomalies. However, supervised techniques require labeled data, which may not always be available or costly to obtain, and they may struggle to generalize to new or unseen types of anomalies not present in the training data.

Unsupervised Anomaly Detection Techniques: Unsupervised anomaly detection techniques do not require labeled data and instead rely solely on the inherent structure and characteristics of the data to identify anomalies. These techniques aim to model the normal behavior of the data and flag instances that deviate significantly from this expected behavior as anomalies.

One popular unsupervised approach is clustering-based anomaly detection, where anomalies are identified as data points that do not belong to any of the identified clusters or exhibit unusual patterns compared to the majority of the data.

CLI command to perform unsupervised anomaly detection using clustering-based techniques in Python using the scikit-learn library:

pythonCopy code

```
from sklearn.cluster import DBSCAN # Initialize
DBSCAN clustering algorithm dbscan =
DBSCAN(eps=0.5, min_samples=5) # Fit the algorithm
to the data dbscan.fit(X)
```

This command will initialize a DBSCAN clustering algorithm with specified parameters and fit it to the feature matrix X.

Unsupervised anomaly detection techniques offer the advantage of not requiring labeled data, making them more suitable for scenarios where labeled data is scarce or unavailable. They can also be more flexible in detecting novel or previously unseen types of anomalies. However, unsupervised techniques may struggle to distinguish between different types of anomalies or normal variations in the data and may require careful tuning of parameters to achieve optimal performance.

In summary, both supervised and unsupervised anomaly detection techniques play important roles in identifying anomalies and unusual patterns in data. By understanding the differences, advantages, and limitations of each approach, practitioners can choose the most suitable technique based on the availability of labeled data, the nature of the data, and the specific requirements of the application domain.

Chapter 8: Text Mining and Natural Language Processing

Text processing is a fundamental task in natural language processing (NLP) and data analysis, aimed at extracting meaningful information from text data. In this section, we will explore various text processing techniques, including tokenization, stemming, lemmatization, stop word removal, and text vectorization. We will discuss their algorithmic principles, implementation methods, and real-world applications, along with CLI commands or explanations on how to deploy the techniques.

Tokenization: Tokenization is the process of breaking down text into smaller units called tokens, which can be words, phrases, or characters. It serves as the initial step in many text processing tasks, enabling further analysis and manipulation of text data.

One common approach to tokenization is using regular expressions to split text into words or sentences based on predefined patterns.

CLI command to perform tokenization using regular expressions in Python:

pythonCopy code

```
import re # Define regular expression pattern for tokenization pattern = r'\w+' # Tokenize text using regular expression tokens = re.findall(pattern, text)
```

This command will tokenize the input text based on the specified regular expression pattern, extracting words as tokens.

Stemming: Stemming is the process of reducing words to their root or base form, removing suffixes and prefixes to normalize the vocabulary. It helps in reducing the dimensionality of text data and improving the performance of downstream NLP tasks such as text classification and information retrieval.

One popular stemming algorithm is the Porter stemming algorithm, which applies a series of heuristic rules to strip suffixes from words.

CLI command to perform stemming using the NLTK library in Python:

pythonCopy code

```
from nltk.stem import PorterStemmer # Initialize
Porter Stemmer stemmer = PorterStemmer() #
Perform stemming on a word stemmed_word =
stemmer.stem(word)
```

This command will initialize a Porter Stemmer and apply stemming to a word, returning its root form.

Lemmatization: Lemmatization is similar to stemming but aims to derive the canonical form or lemma of a word, considering its meaning and context. It produces valid words that exist in the language dictionary, making it more accurate than stemming.

One commonly used lemmatization technique is the WordNet Lemmatizer, which maps words to their corresponding lemma based on WordNet's lexical database.

CLI command to perform lemmatization using the NLTK library in Python:

pythonCopy code

```
from nltk.stem import WordNetLemmatizer # Initialize WordNet Lemmatizer lemmatizer = WordNetLemmatizer() # Perform lemmatization on a word lemmatized_word = lemmatizer.lemmatize(word)
```

This command will initialize a WordNet Lemmatizer and apply lemmatization to a word, returning its lemma.

Stop Word Removal: Stop words are common words such as "the," "is," and "and" that occur frequently in text but carry little semantic meaning. Removing stop words is a preprocessing step in text analysis to improve the quality of features and reduce noise.

CLI command to remove stop words using the NLTK library in Python:

pythonCopy code

```
from nltk.corpus import stopwords # Get list of stop words for a specific language stop_words = set(stopwords.words('english')) # Remove stop words from text filtered_text = [word for word in tokens if word.lower() not in stop_words]
```

This command will retrieve the list of English stop words from NLTK's corpus and remove them from the tokenized text.

Text Vectorization: Text vectorization is the process of converting text data into numerical representations suitable for machine learning algorithms. It transforms text features into vectors of numerical values, enabling the application of various statistical and machine learning techniques to text data.

One common text vectorization technique is the Bag-of-Words (BoW) model, which represents text documents as vectors of word frequencies or presence/absence indicators.

CLI command to perform text vectorization using the CountVectorizer in Python:

pythonCopy code

```
from sklearn.feature_extraction.text import CountVectorizer # Initialize CountVectorizer vectorizer = CountVectorizer() # Fit and transform text data into a document-term matrix X = vectorizer.fit_transform(corpus)
```

This command will initialize a CountVectorizer and fit-transform the corpus of text documents into a document-term matrix, where each row represents a document and each column represents a word in the vocabulary.

In summary, text processing techniques play a crucial role in extracting useful information from text data and preparing it for further analysis or machine learning tasks. By understanding and deploying tokenization, stemming, lemmatization, stop word removal, and text vectorization techniques, practitioners can effectively preprocess text data and extract meaningful insights from diverse text sources, including documents, emails, social media posts, and more.

Sentiment analysis, also known as opinion mining, is a powerful technique in natural language processing (NLP) and data analysis aimed at understanding the sentiments expressed in textual data. In this section, we will delve into the principles, methods, applications, and challenges of sentiment analysis, including sentiment classification, sentiment lexicons, machine learning approaches, and real-world applications, along with CLI commands or explanations on how to deploy the techniques.

Sentiment Classification: Sentiment classification is the task of automatically categorizing text documents or sentences into predefined sentiment classes, such as positive, negative, or neutral. It involves training machine learning models or using rule-based approaches to predict the sentiment polarity of textual data.

One common approach to sentiment classification is using supervised learning algorithms, such as support vector machines (SVMs), naive Bayes, or deep learning models like recurrent neural networks (RNNs) or convolutional neural networks (CNNs).

CLI command to train a sentiment classification model using a naive Bayes classifier in Python with scikit-learn:

pythonCopy code

```
from sklearn.naive_bayes import MultinomialNB from sklearn.feature_extraction.text import TfidfVectorizer # Initialize TF-IDF vectorizer vectorizer = TfidfVectorizer() # Transform text data into TF-IDF
```

features X_train = vectorizer.fit_transform(train_data) # Initialize Multinomial Naive Bayes classifier nb_classifier = MultinomialNB() # Fit the classifier to the training data nb_classifier.fit(X_train, y_train)

This command will initialize a TF-IDF vectorizer to convert text data into numerical features, and then train a Multinomial Naive Bayes classifier on the training data.

Sentiment Lexicons: Sentiment lexicons are curated lists of words or phrases annotated with sentiment polarity labels, indicating their positive, negative, or neutral sentiments. These lexicons serve as valuable resources for sentiment analysis tasks, allowing the identification of sentiment-bearing words in text data. One popular sentiment lexicon is the AFINN lexicon, which assigns numerical sentiment scores to words based on their sentiment polarity.

CLI command to analyze sentiment using the AFINN lexicon in Python:

pythonCopy code

from afinn import Afinn # Initialize AFINN sentiment analyzer afinn = Afinn() # Analyze sentiment of text sentiment_score = afinn.score(text)

This command will initialize an AFINN sentiment analyzer and compute the sentiment score of the input text based on the sentiment polarity of individual words.

Machine Learning Approaches: In addition to supervised learning algorithms, machine learning approaches to sentiment analysis also include unsupervised techniques such as topic modeling, clustering, or rule-based methods.

Topic modeling algorithms like Latent Dirichlet Allocation (LDA) or Non-Negative Matrix Factorization (NMF) can uncover latent topics in text data, which may correlate with specific sentiments expressed by users.

CLI command to perform sentiment analysis using Latent Dirichlet Allocation (LDA) in Python with the Gensim library:

pythonCopy code

```
from gensim.models import LdaModel from gensim.corpora import Dictionary # Tokenize text and create a dictionary of words texts = [text.split() for text in corpus] dictionary = Dictionary(texts) # Convert text data into bag-of-words representation corpus_bow = [dictionary.doc2bow(text) for text in texts] # Initialize LDA model lda_model = LdaModel(corpus_bow, num_topics=3, id2word=dictionary) # Get sentiment topics from the LDA model sentiment_topics = lda_model.show_topics()
```

This command will tokenize text data, create a dictionary of words, convert text into bag-of-words representation, initialize an LDA model with three topics, and extract sentiment topics from the model.

Real-World Applications: Sentiment analysis finds applications in various domains, including social media monitoring, brand reputation management, customer feedback analysis, market research, and product reviews analysis.

CLI command to analyze sentiment of social media posts using the TextBlob library in Python:

pythonCopy code

```
from textblob import TextBlob # Initialize TextBlob sentiment analysis blob = TextBlob(text) # Get sentiment polarity of text sentiment_polarity = blob.sentiment.polarity
```

This command will initialize a TextBlob sentiment analyzer and compute the sentiment polarity of the input text.

In summary, sentiment analysis is a valuable technique for extracting opinions and sentiments from textual data, enabling businesses and organizations to gain insights into customer opinions, market trends, and brand perceptions. By leveraging sentiment classification, sentiment lexicons, machine learning approaches, and real-world applications, practitioners can effectively analyze sentiment in diverse text sources and make data-driven decisions to improve products, services, and customer experiences.

Chapter 9: Web Mining

Web content mining is a process of extracting useful information and knowledge from the vast amount of unstructured data available on the World Wide Web. It involves techniques such as web scraping, web crawling, text extraction, and data preprocessing to transform raw web data into structured and actionable insights. In this section, we will delve into the principles, methods, tools, and applications of web content mining, along with CLI commands or explanations on how to deploy the techniques.

Web Scraping: Web scraping is the automated extraction of data from websites, typically performed by writing scripts or using specialized tools to navigate web pages, extract specific elements, and store the data for analysis.

CLI command to scrape web content using Python with the BeautifulSoup library:

pythonCopy code

```
import requests from bs4 import BeautifulSoup # Send a GET request to the URL response = requests.get(url) # Parse the HTML content of the web page soup = BeautifulSoup(response.content, 'html.parser') # Extract specific elements from the web page title = soup.find('title').get_text() paragraphs = soup.find_all('p') # Print the extracted data print("Title:", title) for paragraph in paragraphs: print("Paragraph:", paragraph.get_text())
```

This command will send a GET request to the specified URL, parse the HTML content using BeautifulSoup, extract the title and paragraphs from the web page, and print the extracted data.

Web Crawling: Web crawling is the systematic process of navigating through web pages and following hyperlinks to discover and retrieve web content from multiple websites. It is often used by search engines to index web pages and build their search databases.

CLI command to crawl web content using the Scrapy framework in Python:

bashCopy code

```
scrapy startproject myproject cd myproject scrapy genspider myspider example.com scrapy crawl myspider
```

This series of commands will create a new Scrapy project, generate a spider for crawling the specified website, and initiate the crawling process.

Text Extraction: Text extraction is the process of isolating and extracting textual content from web pages, removing HTML tags, scripts, and other non-textual elements to focus solely on the textual information.

CLI command to extract text from web pages using the Python library Goose3:

pythonCopy code

```
from goose3 import Goose # Initialize Goose text extractor g = Goose() # Extract text content from the web page article = g.extract(url) # Print the extracted text print("Title:", article.title) print("Text:", article.cleaned_text[:500]) # Print first 500 characters of the extracted text
```

This command will initialize a Goose text extractor, extract the title and textual content from the specified URL, and print the extracted text.

Data Preprocessing: Data preprocessing is a crucial step in web content mining, involving tasks such as text cleaning, normalization, tokenization, and filtering to prepare the extracted data for analysis.

CLI command to preprocess text data using Python with the NLTK library:

pythonCopy code

```
from nltk.tokenize import word_tokenize from nltk.corpus import stopwords from nltk.stem import WordNetLemmatizer import re # Tokenize text tokens = word_tokenize(text) # Remove punctuation and special characters tokens = [word for word in tokens if word.isalnum()] # Convert tokens to lowercase tokens = [word.lower() for word in tokens] # Remove stop words stop_words = set(stopwords.words('english')) tokens = [word for word in tokens if word not in stop_words] # Lemmatize tokens lemmatizer = WordNetLemmatizer() tokens = [lemmatizer.lemmatize(word) for word in tokens] # Print the preprocessed tokens print("Preprocessed Tokens:", tokens)
```

This command will tokenize the text, remove punctuation and special characters, convert tokens to lowercase, remove stop words, lemmatize tokens, and print the preprocessed tokens.

In summary, web content mining enables organizations and researchers to extract valuable insights from the vast amount of information available on the web. By employing techniques such as web scraping, web crawling, text extraction, and data preprocessing, practitioners can gather, analyze, and utilize web data to support various applications, including market research, sentiment analysis, trend detection, and business intelligence.

Web structure mining and usage mining are two essential components of web mining, focusing on the analysis of the structure and usage patterns of the World Wide Web, respectively. In this section, we will explore the principles, methods, tools, and applications of web structure mining and usage mining, along with CLI commands or explanations on how to deploy the techniques.

Web Structure Mining: Web structure mining involves the analysis of the hyperlink structure of the World Wide Web, aiming to uncover patterns, relationships, and properties of web pages and websites. It encompasses techniques such as link analysis, web graph analysis, and page ranking algorithms to understand the organization and connectivity of web resources.

CLI command to perform web structure mining using the PageRank algorithm in Python with NetworkX library:

pythonCopy code

```
import networkx as nx # Create a directed graph
representing web pages and hyperlinks G = nx.DiGraph()
# Add nodes (web pages) G.add_nodes_from(["page1",
"page2", "page3"]) # Add edges (hyperlinks)
G.add_edges_from([("page1", "page2"), ("page1",
"page3"), ("page2", "page3"), ("page3", "page1")]) #
```

Compute PageRank scores for web pages pagerank_scores = nx.pagerank(G) # Print PageRank scores print("PageRank Scores:", pagerank_scores)

This command will create a directed graph representing web pages and hyperlinks, compute PageRank scores for each page, and print the PageRank scores.

Usage Mining: Usage mining focuses on analyzing user interactions and behavior patterns on websites, aiming to understand how users navigate through web pages, access content, and interact with web applications. It involves techniques such as sessionization, clickstream analysis, and association rule mining to extract valuable insights from user logs and clickstream data.

CLI command to perform clickstream analysis using Python with Pandas library:

pythonCopy code

```
import pandas as pd # Read clickstream data from CSV file clickstream_data = pd.read_csv('clickstream_data.csv') # Group clickstream data by session ID session_data = clickstream_data.groupby('session_id') # Compute session duration for each session session_duration = session_data['timestamp'].max() - session_data['timestamp'].min() # Print session duration statistics print("Session Duration Statistics:") print(session_duration.describe())
```

This command will read clickstream data from a CSV file, group the data by session ID, compute the session duration for each session, and print session duration statistics.

Web Structure Mining Applications: Web structure mining finds applications in various domains, including search engine optimization (SEO), web navigation analysis, recommendation systems, and information retrieval. By analyzing the link structure of the web, organizations can improve website navigation, enhance user experience, and optimize content delivery.

CLI command to analyze website structure using Python with BeautifulSoup library:

pythonCopy code

```
from bs4 import BeautifulSoup # Parse HTML content of website soup = BeautifulSoup(html_content, 'html.parser') # Extract hyperlinks from web page hyperlinks = soup.find_all('a', href=True) # Print hyperlinks for link in hyperlinks: print("Hyperlink:", link['href'])
```

This command will parse the HTML content of a website, extract hyperlinks from the web page, and print the hyperlinks.

Usage Mining Applications: Usage mining is widely applied in e-commerce, online advertising, user behavior analysis, and personalized recommendation systems. By analyzing user interactions and clickstream data, organizations can optimize website design, target advertising campaigns, and personalize content recommendations to enhance user engagement and satisfaction.

CLI command to analyze user behavior using Python with scikit-learn library:

pythonCopy code

```
from sklearn.cluster import KMeans # Perform K-means
clustering on clickstream data kmeans =
KMeans(n_clusters=3) clusters =
kmeans.fit_predict(clickstream_data[['time_on_page',
'page_views']]) # Print cluster centers print("Cluster
Centers:") print(kmeans.cluster_centers_)
```

This command will perform K-means clustering on clickstream data, cluster users based on their time on page and number of page views, and print the cluster centers.

In summary, web structure mining and usage mining are vital components of web mining, enabling organizations to extract valuable insights from the structure and usage patterns of the World Wide Web. By employing techniques such as link analysis, clickstream analysis, and association rule mining, practitioners can gain a deeper understanding of web resources, user behavior, and interaction patterns, leading to informed decision-making and improved web experiences.

Chapter 10: Applications of Data Mining in Industry

Data mining plays a pivotal role in the financial industry, offering insights, predictions, and solutions to complex problems. In this section, we will delve into the principles, methods, tools, and applications of data mining in finance, exploring how financial institutions leverage data mining techniques to extract valuable knowledge from large datasets and make informed decisions.

Predictive Modeling: Predictive modeling is a fundamental data mining technique in finance, involving the development of mathematical models to predict future outcomes based on historical data. Financial institutions use predictive modeling for various purposes, including credit scoring, risk assessment, and stock price prediction.

CLI command to train a predictive model using Python with scikit-learn library:

pythonCopy code

```
from sklearn.model_selection import train_test_split from sklearn.ensemble import RandomForestClassifier from sklearn.metrics import accuracy_score # Split data into training and testing sets X_train, X_test, y_train, y_test = train_test_split(features, target, test_size=0.2, random_state=42) # Initialize Random Forest classifier rf_classifier = RandomForestClassifier() # Train the classifier on the training data rf_classifier.fit(X_train,
```

y_train) # Make predictions on the testing data predictions = rf_classifier.predict(X_test) # Evaluate model accuracy accuracy = accuracy_score(y_test, predictions) print("Model Accuracy:", accuracy)

This command will split the data into training and testing sets, initialize a Random Forest classifier, train the classifier on the training data, make predictions on the testing data, and evaluate the model accuracy.

Fraud Detection: Fraud detection is a critical application of data mining in finance, aiming to identify and prevent fraudulent activities such as credit card fraud, money laundering, and insider trading. Financial institutions deploy sophisticated data mining techniques to detect anomalous patterns and deviations from normal behavior.

CLI command to detect fraudulent transactions using Python with the PyOD library:

pythonCopy code

```
from pyod.models.auto_encoder import AutoEncoder
# Initialize AutoEncoder model model = AutoEncoder(hidden_neurons=[10, 2, 2, 10]) # Fit the model to the data model.fit(data) # Predict anomaly scores for transactions anomaly_scores = model.decision_function(data) # Identify fraudulent transactions based on anomaly scores fraudulent_transactions = data[anomaly_scores > threshold]
```

This command will initialize an AutoEncoder model, fit the model to the transaction data, predict anomaly scores for transactions, and identify fraudulent transactions based on a specified threshold.

Customer Segmentation: Customer segmentation is a data mining technique used by financial institutions to group customers into distinct segments based on common characteristics, behaviors, or demographics. By segmenting customers, banks and investment firms can tailor their products, services, and marketing strategies to specific customer segments, enhancing customer satisfaction and retention.

CLI command to perform customer segmentation using Python with the K-means clustering algorithm:

pythonCopy code

```
from sklearn.cluster import KMeans # Initialize K-means clustering algorithm kmeans = KMeans(n_clusters=3) # Fit the algorithm to the customer data kmeans.fit(customer_data) # Assign cluster labels to customers customer_data['cluster'] = kmeans.labels_
```

This command will initialize a K-means clustering algorithm, fit the algorithm to the customer data, and assign cluster labels to customers based on their characteristics.

Portfolio Optimization: Portfolio optimization is a data mining technique used in investment management to construct and manage investment portfolios with the aim of maximizing returns while minimizing risks. Data mining algorithms analyze historical market data, asset correlations, and risk factors to identify optimal portfolio allocations and investment strategies.

CLI command to optimize investment portfolios using Python with the PyPortfolioOpt library:

pythonCopy code

```
from pypfopt.efficient_frontier import EfficientFrontier from pypfopt import risk_models from pypfopt import expected_returns # Calculate expected returns and sample covariance matrix of asset returns mu = expected_returns.mean_historical_return(prices) S = risk_models.sample_cov(prices) # Initialize Efficient Frontier optimizer ef = EfficientFrontier(mu, S) # Optimize portfolio for maximum Sharpe ratio weights = ef.max_sharpe() # Print optimal portfolio weights print("Optimal Portfolio Weights:", weights)
```

This command will calculate the expected returns and sample covariance matrix of asset returns, initialize an Efficient Frontier optimizer, optimize the portfolio for maximum Sharpe ratio, and print the optimal portfolio weights.

In summary, data mining plays a crucial role in the finance industry, enabling financial institutions to extract valuable insights, mitigate risks, detect fraud, and optimize investment decisions. By leveraging predictive modeling, fraud detection techniques, customer segmentation, and portfolio optimization algorithms, organizations can make data-driven decisions, improve operational efficiency, and deliver superior financial services to clients.

Data mining has emerged as a powerful tool in the healthcare industry, enabling healthcare providers, researchers, and policymakers to extract valuable insights from vast amounts of medical data. In this section, we will explore the principles, methods, tools, and applications of data mining in healthcare, examining how it is used to improve patient care, enhance medical research, and optimize healthcare operations.

Predictive Analytics: Predictive analytics is a key application of data mining in healthcare, involving the development of predictive models to forecast patient outcomes, identify at-risk populations, and personalize treatment plans. Healthcare organizations use predictive analytics to predict disease progression, estimate patient readmission rates, and optimize resource allocation.

CLI command to train a predictive model for disease prediction using Python with the scikit-learn library:

pythonCopy code

```
from sklearn.model_selection import train_test_split
from sklearn.ensemble import RandomForestClassifier from sklearn.metrics import accuracy_score # Split data into training and testing sets X_train, X_test, y_train, y_test = train_test_split(features, target, test_size=0.2, random_state=42) # Initialize Random Forest classifier rf_classifier = RandomForestClassifier() # Train the classifier on the training data rf_classifier.fit(X_train, y_train) # Make predictions on the testing data predictions = rf_classifier.predict(X_test) # Evaluate
```

model accuracy accuracy = accuracy_score(y_test, predictions) print("Model Accuracy:", accuracy)

This command will split the data into training and testing sets, initialize a Random Forest classifier, train the classifier on the training data, make predictions on the testing data, and evaluate the model accuracy.

Disease Surveillance: Disease surveillance is another important application of data mining in healthcare, involving the monitoring and analysis of disease patterns, outbreaks, and trends. Healthcare organizations use disease surveillance systems to track the spread of infectious diseases, detect outbreaks in real-time, and implement timely interventions to mitigate the impact of epidemics.

CLI command to analyze disease patterns using Python with the Pandas library:

pythonCopy code

```
import pandas as pd # Read disease data from CSV file disease_data = pd.read_csv('disease_data.csv') # Group disease data by location and time disease_counts = disease_data.groupby(['location', 'date']).size() # Plot disease counts over time for a specific location disease_counts.loc['New York'].plot(title='Disease Counts in New York Over Time')
```

This command will read disease data from a CSV file, group the data by location and time, and plot the disease counts over time for a specific location.

Personalized Medicine: Personalized medicine is a burgeoning field in healthcare that leverages data mining techniques to tailor medical treatments and interventions to individual patients based on their genetic makeup, lifestyle, and medical history. By analyzing patient data, including genomic data, electronic health records (EHRs), and clinical trial data, healthcare providers can develop personalized treatment plans that optimize patient outcomes and minimize adverse effects.

CLI command to analyze genomic data using Python with the Biopython library:

pythonCopy code

```
from Bio import SeqIO # Read genomic data from FASTA file sequences = SeqIO.parse('genome.fasta', 'fasta') # Perform sequence alignment alignment = pairwise2.align.globalxx(sequences[0], sequences[1]) # Print sequence alignment results print("Sequence Alignment:")
print(pairwise2.format_alignment(*alignment[0]))
```

This command will read genomic data from a FASTA file, perform sequence alignment using the globalxx algorithm, and print the sequence alignment results.

Clinical Decision Support: Clinical decision support systems (CDSS) leverage data mining techniques to provide healthcare professionals with evidence-based recommendations, guidelines, and alerts at the point of care. CDSS analyze patient data, medical literature, and best practice guidelines to assist clinicians in making informed decisions regarding diagnosis, treatment, and patient management.

CLI command to deploy a clinical decision support system using Python with the Flask web framework:
pythonCopy code

```
from flask import Flask, request, jsonify app = Flask(__name__) @app.route('/diagnosis', methods=['POST']) def diagnose_patient(): # Extract patient data from request patient_data = request.json # Perform diagnosis using data mining model diagnosis = diagnose_patient(patient_data) # Return diagnosis as JSON response return jsonify(diagnosis) if __name__ == '__main__': app.run(debug=True)
```

This command will deploy a clinical decision support system as a web service using the Flask web framework, allowing clinicians to submit patient data via HTTP POST requests and receive diagnostic recommendations in JSON format.

In summary, data mining plays a crucial role in transforming healthcare by enabling the analysis of large and diverse datasets to extract actionable insights, improve patient outcomes, and optimize healthcare delivery. By leveraging predictive analytics, disease surveillance, personalized medicine, and clinical decision support systems, healthcare organizations can harness the power of data to address complex healthcare challenges and deliver high-quality, patient-centered care.

BOOK 3
ADVANCED DATA SCIENCE
HARNESSING MACHINE LEARNING FOR BIG DATA
ANALYSIS

ROB BOTWRIGHT

Chapter 1: Introduction to Advanced Data Science

Data science has become a cornerstone of modern industry, driving innovation, efficiency, and competitiveness across various sectors. In this section, we will explore the pivotal role of data science in industry, examining its applications, challenges, and future prospects.

Predictive Maintenance: Predictive maintenance is a prominent application of data science in industry, involving the use of advanced analytics and machine learning algorithms to predict equipment failures and schedule maintenance activities proactively. By analyzing sensor data, equipment performance metrics, and maintenance records, industries can reduce downtime, optimize maintenance costs, and improve asset reliability.

CLI command to deploy a predictive maintenance model using Python with the scikit-learn library:

pythonCopy code

```
from sklearn.ensemble import RandomForestClassifier from sklearn.metrics import accuracy_score # Initialize Random Forest classifier rf_classifier = RandomForestClassifier() # Train the classifier on historical maintenance data rf_classifier.fit(X_train, y_train) # Make predictions for future maintenance events predictions = rf_classifier.predict(X_test) # Evaluate model accuracy
```

```
accuracy = accuracy_score(y_test, predictions)
print("Model Accuracy:", accuracy)
```
This command will initialize a Random Forest classifier, train the classifier on historical maintenance data, make predictions for future maintenance events, and evaluate the model accuracy.

Supply Chain Optimization: Data science plays a crucial role in optimizing supply chain operations, enabling industries to streamline inventory management, improve demand forecasting, and enhance logistics efficiency. By analyzing historical sales data, market trends, and supplier performance metrics, companies can make data-driven decisions to reduce costs, minimize stockouts, and meet customer demands more effectively.

CLI command to optimize inventory levels using Python with the Pandas library:

pythonCopy code

```
import pandas as pd # Read sales and inventory data from CSV files sales_data = pd.read_csv('sales_data.csv') inventory_data = pd.read_csv('inventory_data.csv') # Merge sales and inventory data merged_data = pd.merge(sales_data, inventory_data, on='product_id') # Calculate inventory turnover ratio for each product merged_data['inventory_turnover'] = merged_data['sales_volume'] / merged_data['inventory_level'] # Identify slow-moving products with low inventory turnover
```

slow_moving_products   =
merged_data[merged_data['inventory_turnover'] < 1]
This command will read sales and inventory data from
CSV files, merge the data, calculate the inventory
turnover ratio for each product, and identify slow-
moving products with low inventory turnover.

Customer Segmentation and Personalization: Data
science enables industries to segment customers into
distinct groups based on their behavior, preferences,
and demographics, allowing companies to personalize
products, services, and marketing campaigns to
specific customer segments. By analyzing customer
transaction data, browsing history, and social media
interactions, businesses can create targeted
marketing strategies that enhance customer
engagement and loyalty.

CLI command to perform customer segmentation
using Python with the K-means clustering algorithm:
pythonCopy code

```
from sklearn.cluster import KMeans # Initialize K-
means clustering algorithm kmeans =
KMeans(n_clusters=3) # Fit the algorithm to customer
transaction data kmeans.fit(customer_data) # Assign
cluster labels to customers customer_data['cluster'] =
kmeans.labels_
```

This command will initialize a K-means clustering
algorithm, fit the algorithm to customer transaction
data, and assign cluster labels to customers based on
their characteristics.

Quality Control and Process Optimization: Data science techniques are instrumental in improving product quality and optimizing manufacturing processes in industry. By analyzing sensor data, production metrics, and defect records, industries can detect anomalies, identify root causes of quality issues, and implement corrective actions to enhance product quality, reduce waste, and increase productivity.

CLI command to analyze sensor data using Python with the NumPy library:

pythonCopy code

```python
import numpy as np # Load sensor data from CSV file
sensor_data = np.loadtxt('sensor_data.csv', delimiter=',') # Calculate mean and standard deviation of sensor readings mean = np.mean(sensor_data)
std_dev = np.std(sensor_data) # Identify outliers in sensor data outliers = sensor_data[np.abs(sensor_data - mean) > 3 * std_dev]
```

This command will load sensor data from a CSV file, calculate the mean and standard deviation of sensor readings, and identify outliers in the sensor data.

In summary, data science has revolutionized modern industry by enabling companies to harness the power of data to drive innovation, optimize operations, and gain a competitive edge. Through applications such as predictive maintenance, supply chain optimization, customer segmentation, and quality control, industries can unlock valuable insights from data to make informed decisions, improve efficiency, and deliver greater value to customers.

As data science continues to evolve rapidly, driven by technological advancements and increasing data complexity, it is essential to explore the latest trends and challenges shaping the field. In this section, we will delve into the emerging trends and key challenges in advanced data science, providing insights into the future direction of the discipline.

Artificial Intelligence and Machine Learning: Artificial intelligence (AI) and machine learning (ML) are at the forefront of advanced data science, driving innovations in predictive analytics, natural language processing, and computer vision. The proliferation of deep learning models, fueled by advancements in neural network architectures and computational resources, has enabled breakthroughs in image recognition, speech synthesis, and autonomous systems.

CLI command to train a deep learning model using Python with the TensorFlow library:

pythonCopy code

```
import tensorflow as tf # Define and compile a convolutional neural network (CNN) model model = tf.keras.Sequential([ tf.keras.layers.Conv2D(32, (3, 3), activation='relu', input_shape=(28, 28, 1)), tf.keras.layers.MaxPooling2D((2, 2)), tf.keras.layers.Flatten(), tf.keras.layers.Dense(128, activation='relu'), tf.keras.layers.Dense(10, activation='softmax') ])
```

```python
model.compile(optimizer='adam',
loss='sparse_categorical_crossentropy',
metrics=['accuracy']) # Train the model on training
data model.fit(train_images, train_labels, epochs=10)
```
This command will define and compile a convolutional neural network (CNN) model using TensorFlow, and train the model on training data.

Big Data Analytics and Scalability: The exponential growth of data volume, velocity, and variety presents significant challenges and opportunities for advanced data science. Big data analytics frameworks such as Apache Hadoop and Apache Spark enable the processing and analysis of massive datasets distributed across clusters of commodity hardware. However, ensuring scalability, fault tolerance, and efficient resource utilization remains a key challenge in deploying large-scale data analytics solutions.

CLI command to deploy a Spark job for distributed data processing:

bashCopy code

```bash
spark-submit --class com.example.DataProcessingApp
--master spark://master-node:7077 data-processing.jar
```

This command will submit a Spark job for distributed data processing to the Spark cluster, executing the specified application class defined in the data-processing.jar file.

Explainable AI and Ethical Considerations: As AI and ML models become more pervasive in decision-making processes across various domains, there is a growing demand for explainable AI (XAI) techniques that provide insights into model predictions and decision rationale. Interpretable machine learning models and model-agnostic explainability techniques enable stakeholders to understand, trust, and validate model outputs, ensuring transparency and accountability in AI-driven systems. Additionally, addressing ethical considerations such as bias, fairness, and privacy is crucial to building responsible AI solutions that prioritize societal values and respect individual rights.

CLI command to analyze model explanations using Python with the LIME library:

pythonCopy code

```
from lime.lime_tabular import LimeTabularExplainer
# Initialize LIME explainer for interpreting model predictions              explainer              =
LimeTabularExplainer(training_data,
mode='regression')  #  Explain  a  single  instance
prediction     using     LIME     explanation     =
explainer.explain_instance(instance, model.predict)
```

This command will initialize a LIME explainer for interpreting model predictions based on tabular data, and generate explanations for a single instance prediction using the trained model.

Edge Computing and IoT Integration: The proliferation of Internet of Things (IoT) devices and sensors has led to the generation of vast amounts of real-time data at the network edge. Edge computing technologies enable data processing and analysis to be performed closer to the data source, reducing latency, conserving bandwidth, and enhancing privacy. Advanced data science techniques such as federated learning and edge analytics empower organizations to leverage distributed data resources efficiently while addressing challenges related to data privacy, security, and regulatory compliance.

CLI command to deploy a federated learning model for edge devices:

bashCopy code

```
docker run --rm --privileged multi-platform/buildpack-deps:latest-docker -- docker build -t edge-learning-model -f Dockerfile . docker run --rm -d -p 5000:5000 edge-learning-model
```

These commands will build a Docker image for deploying a federated learning model for edge devices, and run a containerized instance of the model API on port 5000.

In summary, advanced data science continues to evolve rapidly, driven by emerging technologies, evolving data landscapes, and evolving societal needs. By embracing trends such as AI and ML innovation, big data analytics scalability, explainable AI, ethical considerations, edge computing, and IoT integration, organizations can unlock new opportunities, overcome challenges, and harness the power of data to drive innovation, improve decision-making, and create value in the digital era.

Chapter 2: Fundamentals of Machine Learning

Machine learning, a subfield of artificial intelligence, has gained immense popularity in recent years for its ability to enable computers to learn from data and make predictions or decisions without being explicitly programmed. In this section, we will delve into the fundamental concepts of machine learning, providing insights into its core principles, techniques, and applications.

Supervised Learning: Supervised learning is one of the fundamental paradigms in machine learning, where the algorithm learns from labeled data, consisting of input-output pairs, to make predictions or infer relationships between variables. In supervised learning, the algorithm aims to learn a mapping function that maps input features to corresponding output labels, allowing it to generalize to unseen data and make accurate predictions.

CLI command to train a supervised learning model using Python with the scikit-learn library:

pythonCopy code

```
from sklearn.linear_model import LinearRegression
from sklearn.model_selection import train_test_split
from sklearn.metrics import mean_squared_error #
Split data into training and testing sets X_train, X_test,
y_train, y_test = train_test_split(features, target,
test_size=0.2, random_state=42) # Initialize and train a
linear regression model model = LinearRegression()
model.fit(X_train, y_train) # Make predictions on the
```

testing set predictions = model.predict(X_test) # Evaluate model performance using mean squared error mse = mean_squared_error(y_test, predictions) print("Mean Squared Error:", mse)

This command will split the data into training and testing sets, initialize and train a linear regression model on the training data, make predictions on the testing set, and evaluate the model performance using mean squared error.

Unsupervised Learning: Unsupervised learning is another fundamental paradigm in machine learning, where the algorithm learns patterns and structures from unlabeled data without explicit supervision. In unsupervised learning, the algorithm aims to discover hidden patterns, relationships, or groupings within the data, enabling tasks such as clustering, dimensionality reduction, and anomaly detection.

CLI command to perform clustering using Python with the scikit-learn library:

pythonCopy code

```
from sklearn.cluster import KMeans from sklearn.preprocessing import StandardScaler import matplotlib.pyplot as plt # Standardize the feature matrix scaler = StandardScaler() scaled_features = scaler.fit_transform(features) # Initialize and fit a K-means clustering model kmeans = KMeans(n_clusters=3) kmeans.fit(scaled_features) # Visualize the clustering results plt.scatter(features[:, 0], features[:, 1], c=kmeans.labels_, cmap='viridis') plt.scatter(kmeans.cluster_centers_[:, 0], kmeans.cluster_centers_[:, 1], marker='x', color='red')
```

plt.xlabel('Feature 1') plt.ylabel('Feature 2') plt.title('K-means Clustering') plt.show()

This command will standardize the feature matrix, initialize and fit a K-means clustering model to the standardized features, and visualize the clustering results.

Feature Engineering: Feature engineering is a critical aspect of machine learning, involving the selection, transformation, and creation of input features to improve model performance and generalization. Effective feature engineering techniques can enhance model interpretability, reduce overfitting, and capture meaningful relationships between variables.

CLI command to perform feature scaling using Python with the scikit-learn library:

pythonCopy code

```
from sklearn.preprocessing import MinMaxScaler # Initialize Min-Max scaler scaler = MinMaxScaler() # Perform feature scaling on the feature matrix scaled_features = scaler.fit_transform(features)
```

This command will initialize a Min-Max scaler and perform feature scaling on the feature matrix, ensuring that all features are scaled to the same range.

Model Evaluation and Validation: Model evaluation and validation are essential steps in machine learning, allowing practitioners to assess the performance of trained models and ensure their reliability and generalization capability. Common techniques for model evaluation include cross-validation, where the dataset is split into multiple subsets for training and testing, and metrics such as accuracy, precision, recall, and F1-score are used to quantify model performance.

CLI command to perform cross-validation using Python with the scikit-learn library:

pythonCopy code

```
from sklearn.model_selection import cross_val_score
from sklearn.tree import DecisionTreeClassifier # Initialize decision tree classifier clf = DecisionTreeClassifier() # Perform 5-fold cross-validation scores = cross_val_score(clf, features, target, cv=5) # Print mean accuracy and standard deviation of scores print("Mean Accuracy:", scores.mean()) print("Standard Deviation of Accuracy:", scores.std())
```

This command will initialize a decision tree classifier, perform 5-fold cross-validation on the dataset using the classifier, and print the mean accuracy and standard deviation of the cross-validation scores.

In summary, understanding the basic concepts of machine learning is crucial for building effective and reliable predictive models. By mastering supervised and unsupervised learning techniques, feature engineering, and model evaluation and validation, practitioners can develop robust machine learning solutions that address real-world problems and drive innovation across various domains.

Machine learning algorithms form the backbone of data-driven decision-making processes, enabling computers to learn from data and make predictions or decisions without explicit programming. In this section, we will explore the various types of machine learning algorithms, each tailored to address different types of learning tasks and data characteristics.

Supervised Learning Algorithms: Supervised learning algorithms learn from labeled data, where the input features are associated with corresponding output labels or target variables. These algorithms are trained on historical data with known outcomes, allowing them to make predictions or infer relationships between input features and output labels.

CLI command to train a supervised learning model using Python with the scikit-learn library:

pythonCopy code

```
from sklearn.linear_model import LinearRegression
from sklearn.model_selection import train_test_split
from sklearn.metrics import mean_squared_error # Split data into training and testing sets X_train, X_test, y_train, y_test = train_test_split(features, target, test_size=0.2, random_state=42) # Initialize and train a linear regression model model = LinearRegression() model.fit(X_train, y_train) # Make predictions on the testing set predictions = model.predict(X_test) # Evaluate model performance using mean squared error mse = mean_squared_error(y_test, predictions) print("Mean Squared Error:", mse)
```

This command will split the data into training and testing sets, initialize and train a linear regression model on the training data, make predictions on the testing set, and evaluate the model performance using mean squared error.

Unsupervised Learning Algorithms: Unsupervised learning algorithms learn from unlabeled data, where the input features are not associated with any specific output labels or target variables. These algorithms aim to discover patterns, structures, or groupings within the data, enabling tasks such as clustering, dimensionality reduction, and anomaly detection.

CLI command to perform clustering using Python with the scikit-learn library:

pythonCopy code

```
from sklearn.cluster import KMeans from sklearn.preprocessing import StandardScaler import matplotlib.pyplot as plt # Standardize the feature matrix scaler = StandardScaler() scaled_features = scaler.fit_transform(features) # Initialize and fit a K-means clustering model kmeans = KMeans(n_clusters=3) kmeans.fit(scaled_features) # Visualize the clustering results plt.scatter(features[:, 0], features[:, 1], c=kmeans.labels_, cmap='viridis') plt.scatter(kmeans.cluster_centers_[:, 0], kmeans.cluster_centers_[:, 1], marker='x', color='red') plt.xlabel('Feature 1') plt.ylabel('Feature 2') plt.title('K-means Clustering') plt.show()
```

This command will standardize the feature matrix, initialize and fit a K-means clustering model to the standardized features, and visualize the clustering results.

Semi-Supervised Learning Algorithms: Semi-supervised learning algorithms leverage a combination of labeled and unlabeled data for training. These algorithms exploit the abundance of unlabeled data to improve model performance and generalization, especially in scenarios where labeled data is scarce or expensive to obtain.

CLI command to train a semi-supervised learning model using Python with the scikit-learn library:

pythonCopy code

```
from sklearn.semi_supervised import LabelPropagation
from sklearn.metrics import accuracy_score # Initialize and fit a label propagation model model = LabelPropagation() model.fit(features, labels) # Make predictions on the unlabeled data predictions = model.predict(unlabeled_features) # Evaluate model performance using accuracy score accuracy = accuracy_score(true_labels, predictions) print("Accuracy:", accuracy)
```

This command will initialize and fit a label propagation model using both labeled and unlabeled data, make predictions on the unlabeled data, and evaluate the model performance using the accuracy score.

Reinforcement Learning Algorithms: Reinforcement learning algorithms learn through interaction with an environment, where they receive feedback in the form of rewards or penalties based on their actions. These algorithms aim to learn a policy that maximizes cumulative rewards over time, enabling tasks such as game playing, robotics control, and autonomous decision-making.

CLI command to train a reinforcement learning agent using Python with the OpenAI Gym library:

pythonCopy code

```
import gym # Initialize the CartPole environment env = gym.make('CartPole-v1') # Train the agent using the
```

Proximal Policy Optimization (PPO) algorithm model = PPO('MlpPolicy', env, verbose=1) model.learn(total_timesteps=10000) # Evaluate the trained agent's performance mean_reward, _ = evaluate_policy(model, env, n_eval_episodes=10) print("Mean Reward:", mean_reward)

This command will initialize the CartPole environment, train the agent using the Proximal Policy Optimization (PPO) algorithm, and evaluate the trained agent's performance based on the mean reward achieved over multiple evaluation episodes.

In summary, understanding the various types of machine learning algorithms is essential for selecting the most appropriate approach to tackle specific learning tasks and data characteristics. By leveraging supervised, unsupervised, semi-supervised, and reinforcement learning algorithms, practitioners can develop robust machine learning solutions that address a wide range of real-world problems and drive innovation across diverse domains.

Chapter 3: Supervised Learning Techniques

Regression analysis is a statistical technique used to explore the relationship between a dependent variable and one or more independent variables. It aims to model the relationship between variables and make predictions based on observed data. In this section, we will delve into the fundamentals of regression analysis, including its types, applications, and practical implementation.

Linear Regression: Linear regression is one of the most commonly used regression techniques, particularly when the relationship between variables can be approximated by a straight line. It involves fitting a linear equation to the observed data, with the objective of minimizing the difference between the actual and predicted values of the dependent variable.

CLI command to perform linear regression using Python with the scikit-learn library:

pythonCopy code

```
from sklearn.linear_model import LinearRegression
from sklearn.model_selection import train_test_split
from sklearn.metrics import mean_squared_error # Split data into training and testing sets X_train, X_test, y_train, y_test = train_test_split(features, target, test_size=0.2, random_state=42) # Initialize and train a linear regression model model = LinearRegression() model.fit(X_train, y_train) # Make
```

predictions on the testing set predictions = model.predict(X_test) # Evaluate model performance using mean squared error mse = mean_squared_error(y_test, predictions) print("Mean Squared Error:", mse)

This command will split the data into training and testing sets, initialize and train a linear regression model on the training data, make predictions on the testing set, and evaluate the model performance using mean squared error.

Polynomial Regression: Polynomial regression extends the concept of linear regression by fitting a polynomial function to the observed data. It is suitable for modeling non-linear relationships between variables, where the relationship cannot be adequately captured by a straight line.

CLI command to perform polynomial regression using Python with the scikit-learn library:

pythonCopy code

```
from sklearn.preprocessing import PolynomialFeatures # Generate polynomial features poly = PolynomialFeatures(degree=2) X_poly = poly.fit_transform(features) # Split data into training and testing sets X_train, X_test, y_train, y_test = train_test_split(X_poly, target, test_size=0.2, random_state=42) # Initialize and train a linear regression model model = LinearRegression() model.fit(X_train, y_train) # Make predictions on the testing set predictions = model.predict(X_test) # Evaluate model performance using mean squared
```

error mse = mean_squared_error(y_test, predictions) print("Mean Squared Error:", mse)

This command will generate polynomial features up to the specified degree, split the data into training and testing sets, initialize and train a linear regression model on the polynomial features, make predictions on the testing set, and evaluate the model performance using mean squared error.

Ridge Regression: Ridge regression is a regularization technique used to mitigate overfitting in regression models by adding a penalty term to the loss function. It shrinks the coefficients of the regression variables, preventing them from becoming too large and unstable.

CLI command to perform ridge regression using Python with the scikit-learn library:

pythonCopy code

```
from sklearn.linear_model import Ridge # Initialize and train a ridge regression model model = Ridge(alpha=0.1) model.fit(X_train, y_train) # Make predictions on the testing set predictions = model.predict(X_test) # Evaluate model performance using mean squared error mse = mean_squared_error(y_test, predictions) print("Mean Squared Error:", mse)
```

This command will initialize and train a ridge regression model with the specified regularization parameter (alpha), make predictions on the testing set, and evaluate the model performance using mean squared error.

Logistic Regression: Logistic regression is a regression technique used for binary classification tasks, where the dependent variable is categorical and binary (e.g., yes/no, 0/1). It models the probability of the occurrence of a certain event by fitting a logistic function to the observed data.

CLI command to perform logistic regression using Python with the scikit-learn library:

pythonCopy code

```
from sklearn.linear_model import LogisticRegression
# Initialize and train a logistic regression model model = LogisticRegression() model.fit(X_train, y_train) # Make predictions on the testing set predictions = model.predict(X_test) # Evaluate model performance using accuracy score accuracy = accuracy_score(y_test, predictions) print("Accuracy:", accuracy)
```

This command will initialize and train a logistic regression model, make predictions on the testing set, and evaluate the model performance using the accuracy score.

In summary, regression analysis is a powerful statistical technique for modeling and predicting continuous and categorical variables based on observed data. By leveraging various regression techniques such as linear regression, polynomial regression, ridge regression, and logistic regression, practitioners can gain valuable insights into the relationships between variables and make informed decisions in a wide range of domains.

Chapter 4: Unsupervised Learning Methods

Clustering algorithms are unsupervised learning techniques used to group similar data points together based on their characteristics or features. These algorithms enable the discovery of inherent structures or patterns within datasets, facilitating data exploration, pattern recognition, and decision-making processes. In this section, we will explore various clustering algorithms, their applications, and practical implementation.

K-Means Clustering: K-means clustering is one of the most popular and widely used clustering algorithms. It partitions the dataset into K clusters by iteratively assigning data points to the nearest cluster centroid and updating the centroids based on the mean of the data points assigned to each cluster.

CLI command to perform K-means clustering using Python with the scikit-learn library:

pythonCopy code

```
from sklearn.cluster import KMeans # Initialize and fit a K-means clustering model kmeans = KMeans(n_clusters=3) kmeans.fit(features) # Get cluster labels and centroids cluster_labels = kmeans.labels_ centroids = kmeans.cluster_centers_
```

This command will initialize and fit a K-means clustering model with the specified number of clusters (n_clusters), assign cluster labels to each data point, and compute the centroids of the clusters.

Hierarchical Clustering: Hierarchical clustering is a bottom-up or agglomerative clustering technique that creates a dendrogram by iteratively merging the closest data points or clusters until a single cluster containing all data points is formed. It does not require specifying the number of clusters beforehand and enables the visualization of hierarchical relationships.

CLI command to perform hierarchical clustering using Python with the scipy library:

pythonCopy code

```
from scipy.cluster.hierarchy import linkage, dendrogram import matplotlib.pyplot as plt # Compute the linkage matrix using hierarchical clustering linkage_matrix = linkage(features, method='ward') # Plot the dendrogram plt.figure(figsize=(12, 8)) dendrogram(linkage_matrix) plt.xlabel('Data Points') plt.ylabel('Distance') plt.title('Hierarchical Clustering Dendrogram') plt.show()
```

This command will compute the linkage matrix using hierarchical clustering with the Ward method, which minimizes the variance when merging clusters, and plot the resulting dendrogram for visualization.

DBSCAN (Density-Based Spatial Clustering of Applications with Noise): DBSCAN is a density-based clustering algorithm that groups together data points that are closely packed in high-density regions and separates outliers or noise points in low-density regions. It does not require specifying the number of clusters beforehand and is robust to noise and outliers.

CLI command to perform DBSCAN clustering using Python with the scikit-learn library:

pythonCopy code

```
from sklearn.cluster import DBSCAN # Initialize and fit a DBSCAN clustering model dbscan = DBSCAN(eps=0.5, min_samples=5) dbscan.fit(features) # Get cluster labels and noise points cluster_labels = dbscan.labels_ noise_points = features[dbscan.labels_ == -1]
```

This command will initialize and fit a DBSCAN clustering model with the specified maximum distance between samples (eps) and minimum number of samples in a neighborhood (min_samples), assign cluster labels to each data point, and identify noise points as those labeled -1.

Gaussian Mixture Models (GMM): Gaussian Mixture Models assume that the data is generated from a mixture of several Gaussian distributions and estimate the parameters of these distributions to fit the data. They can capture complex cluster shapes and are suitable for datasets with overlapping clusters.

CLI command to perform GMM clustering using Python with the scikit-learn library:

pythonCopy code

```
from sklearn.mixture import GaussianMixture # Initialize and fit a GMM clustering model gmm = GaussianMixture(n_components=3) gmm.fit(features)
```

```
# Get cluster assignments and probabilities
cluster_assignments = gmm.predict(features)
probabilities = gmm.predict_proba(features)
```
This command will initialize and fit a GMM clustering model with the specified number of components (n_components), assign cluster labels to each data point, and compute the probabilities of each data point belonging to each cluster.

In summary, clustering algorithms play a crucial role in exploratory data analysis, pattern recognition, and segmentation tasks across various domains. By understanding the principles and characteristics of different clustering algorithms such as K-means, hierarchical clustering, DBSCAN, and Gaussian Mixture Models, practitioners can effectively analyze and interpret complex datasets, uncover hidden structures, and derive actionable insights for decision-making purposes.

Dimensionality reduction is a fundamental process in data analysis and machine learning that aims to reduce the number of features or variables in a dataset while preserving its essential information and structure. By reducing the dimensionality of the data, we can overcome the curse of dimensionality, improve computational efficiency, and enhance model performance. In this section, we will explore various dimensionality reduction techniques, their applications, and practical implementation.

Principal Component Analysis (PCA): Principal Component Analysis is one of the most commonly used dimensionality reduction techniques. It transforms the original features into a new set of orthogonal variables called principal components, which are linear combinations of the original features. PCA identifies the directions of maximum variance in the data and projects the data onto these principal components, thereby reducing the dimensionality while retaining most of the variance.

CLI command to perform PCA using Python with the scikit-learn library:

pythonCopy code

```
from sklearn.decomposition import PCA # Initialize and fit a PCA model pca = PCA(n_components=2) principal_components = pca.fit_transform(features) # Explained variance ratio explained_variance_ratio = pca.explained_variance_ratio_
```

This command will initialize and fit a PCA model with the specified number of components (n_components), transform the original features into principal components, and compute the explained variance ratio, which indicates the proportion of variance explained by each principal component.

t-Distributed Stochastic Neighbor Embedding (t-SNE): t-SNE is a nonlinear dimensionality reduction technique commonly used for visualization purposes. It maps high-dimensional data to a lower-dimensional space while preserving the local structure and pairwise similarities between data points. t-SNE optimizes a cost function to minimize the divergence between the original pairwise similarities and the similarities in the lower-dimensional embedding.

CLI command to perform t-SNE using Python with the scikit-learn library:

pythonCopy code

```
from sklearn.manifold import TSNE # Initialize and fit a t-SNE model tsne = TSNE(n_components=2, perplexity=30, learning_rate=200) embedded_data = tsne.fit_transform(features)
```

This command will initialize and fit a t-SNE model with the specified number of components (n_components), perplexity, and learning rate, transform the original features into a lower-dimensional embedding, and preserve the local structure and pairwise similarities.

Linear Discriminant Analysis (LDA): Linear Discriminant Analysis is a supervised dimensionality reduction technique commonly used for classification tasks. It identifies the linear combinations of features that best separate the classes in the data. LDA aims to maximize the between-class scatter while minimizing the within-class scatter, resulting in a lower-dimensional space that maximizes class discrimination.

CLI command to perform LDA using Python with the scikit-learn library:

pythonCopy code

```
from sklearn.discriminant_analysis import LinearDiscriminantAnalysis # Initialize and fit an LDA model lda =
```

LinearDiscriminantAnalysis(n_components=2)
lda_components = lda.fit_transform(features, labels)
This command will initialize and fit an LDA model with the specified number of components (n_components), transform the original features into the linear discriminant components, and maximize the class separability in the lower-dimensional space.

Autoencoders: Autoencoders are neural network architectures used for unsupervised dimensionality reduction and feature learning. They consist of an encoder network that compresses the input data into a lower-dimensional representation (encoding) and a decoder network that reconstructs the original input from the encoded representation. Autoencoders learn to capture the essential features of the data and discard the redundant information during the training process.

CLI command to train an autoencoder using Python with the Keras library:

pythonCopy code

```
from keras.layers import Input, Dense from keras.models import Model # Define the input layer input_layer = Input(shape=(input_dim,)) # Define the encoder and decoder layers encoded = Dense(encoding_dim, activation='relu')(input_layer) decoded = Dense(input_dim, activation='sigmoid')(encoded) # Define the autoencoder model autoencoder = Model(input_layer, decoded) # Compile the model autoencoder.compile(optimizer='adam',
```

```
loss='binary_crossentropy') # Train the autoencoder
autoencoder.fit(features, features, epochs=50,
batch_size=256, shuffle=True)
```

This command will define the architecture of the autoencoder model, compile it with the Adam optimizer and binary cross-entropy loss function, and train it on the input features for a specified number of epochs and batch size.

In summary, dimensionality reduction techniques play a crucial role in data preprocessing, visualization, and feature learning tasks in various domains. By understanding the principles and applications of techniques such as PCA, t-SNE, LDA, and autoencoders, practitioners can effectively reduce the dimensionality of high-dimensional datasets, extract meaningful features, and improve the performance of downstream machine learning models.

Chapter 5: Deep Learning and Neural Networks

Deep learning, a subfield of machine learning, has garnered significant attention and revolutionized various industries by enabling computers to learn from large amounts of data and make predictions or decisions without explicit programming. In this section, we will delve into the fundamentals of deep learning, its architecture, training process, and practical applications.

Deep learning models are characterized by their ability to automatically learn hierarchical representations of data through multiple layers of abstraction. These models are typically composed of artificial neural networks with numerous interconnected nodes or neurons organized into layers. Each layer performs specific operations on the input data and passes the transformed information to the next layer, allowing the model to capture complex patterns and relationships in the data.

Neural Network Architecture: The basic building block of a neural network is the neuron, which receives input signals, applies a transformation using weights and biases, and generates an output signal. A neural network consists of an input layer, one or more hidden layers, and an output layer. The input layer receives the raw data, the hidden layers perform computations, and the output layer produces the final predictions or classifications.

CLI command to create a neural network using Python with the TensorFlow library:
pythonCopy code
import tensorflow as tf from tensorflow.keras.models import Sequential from tensorflow.keras.layers import Dense # Define the neural network architecture model = Sequential([Dense(64, activation='relu', input_shape=(input_dim,)), Dense(32, activation='relu'), Dense(num_classes, activation='softmax')]) # Compile the model model.compile(optimizer='adam', loss='sparse_categorical_crossentropy', metrics=['accuracy']) # Train the model model.fit(train_data, train_labels, epochs=10, batch_size=32, validation_data=(val_data, val_labels))

This command will define a neural network model with two hidden layers, using the ReLU activation function for nonlinearity, and the softmax activation function in the output layer for multiclass classification. It will compile the model with the Adam optimizer and sparse categorical cross-entropy loss function and train it on the training data for a specified number of epochs and batch size.

Training Process: The training process of a deep learning model involves feeding it with labeled training data, computing predictions, comparing the predictions with the actual labels, and adjusting the model parameters to minimize the prediction error. This process is known as backpropagation, where the gradients of the loss function with respect to the model parameters are computed and used to update the weights and biases of the network using optimization algorithms such as stochastic gradient descent (SGD) or its variants.

CLI command to train a neural network using Python with the TensorFlow library:

pythonCopy code

```
# Train the model model.fit(train_data, train_labels, epochs=10, batch_size=32, validation_data=(val_data, val_labels))
```

This command will train the compiled neural network model on the labeled training data for a specified number of epochs and batch size, while validating the model's performance on the validation data.

Practical Applications: Deep learning has been applied to a wide range of real-world problems across various domains, including computer vision, natural language processing, speech recognition, healthcare, finance, and autonomous vehicles. Some notable applications include image classification, object detection, sentiment analysis, medical diagnosis, fraud detection, and autonomous driving.

CLI command to deploy a trained deep learning model for inference using Python with the TensorFlow library:

pythonCopy code

```
# Load the trained model model = tf.keras.models.load_model('trained_model.h5')   # Perform inference on new data predictions = model.predict(new_data)
```

This command will load a pre-trained deep learning model saved in the Hierarchical Data Format (HDF5) file format and use it to make predictions on new unseen data.

In summary, deep learning has emerged as a powerful and versatile approach for solving complex problems and extracting valuable insights from large-scale datasets. By understanding the principles of neural network architecture, the training process, and practical applications of deep learning, practitioners can leverage this technology to address various challenges and drive innovation across industries.

Neural networks have witnessed remarkable advancements in recent years, leading to the development of diverse architectures tailored for specific tasks and domains. In this section, we will explore various neural network architectures, their design principles, and practical applications across different fields.

Feedforward Neural Networks (FNN): Feedforward neural networks, also known as multi-layer perceptrons (MLPs), are the simplest form of neural networks consisting of multiple layers of neurons arranged in a feedforward manner. Each neuron in one layer is connected to every neuron in the subsequent layer, and information flows only in one direction, from input to output. FNNs are versatile and widely used for classification and regression tasks in domains such as finance, healthcare, and image recognition.

CLI command to create a feedforward neural network using Python with the TensorFlow library:

pythonCopy code

```
import tensorflow as tf from tensorflow.keras.models import Sequential from tensorflow.keras.layers import Dense # Define the feedforward neural network architecture model = Sequential([ Dense(64, activation='relu', input_shape=(input_dim,)), Dense(32, activation='relu'), Dense(num_classes, activation='softmax') ]) # Compile the model model.compile(optimizer='adam', loss='sparse_categorical_crossentropy', metrics=['accuracy']) # Train the model model.fit(train_data, train_labels, epochs=10, batch_size=32, validation_data=(val_data, val_labels))
```

This command will define a feedforward neural network model with two hidden layers and one output layer, using the ReLU activation function for nonlinearity in the hidden layers and the softmax activation function in the output layer for multiclass classification. It will compile the model with the Adam optimizer and sparse categorical cross-entropy loss function and train it on the labeled training data for a specified number of epochs and batch size.

Convolutional Neural Networks (CNN): Convolutional neural networks are specialized architectures designed for processing structured grid-like data such as images. CNNs consist of convolutional layers followed by pooling layers, which extract hierarchical features from the input data while preserving spatial information. CNNs have achieved state-of-the-art performance in image classification, object detection, and image segmentation tasks.

CLI command to create a convolutional neural network using Python with the TensorFlow library:

pythonCopy code

```
from tensorflow.keras.layers import Conv2D, MaxPooling2D, Flatten # Define the convolutional neural network architecture model = Sequential([ Conv2D(32, kernel_size=(3, 3), activation='relu', input_shape=(img_height, img_width, num_channels)), MaxPooling2D(pool_size=(2, 2)), Conv2D(64, kernel_size=(3, 3), activation='relu'), MaxPooling2D(pool_size=(2, 2)), Flatten(), Dense(128, activation='relu'), Dense(num_classes, activation='softmax') ]) # Compile the model model.compile(optimizer='adam', loss='sparse_categorical_crossentropy', metrics=['accuracy']) # Train the model model.fit(train_images, train_labels, epochs=10, batch_size=32, validation_data=(val_images, val_labels))
```

This command will define a convolutional neural network model with two convolutional layers followed by max-pooling layers for feature extraction and spatial reduction, respectively. The model also includes fully connected layers for classification. It will compile the model with the Adam optimizer and sparse categorical cross-entropy loss function and train it on the labeled image data for a specified number of epochs and batch size.

Recurrent Neural Networks (RNN): Recurrent neural networks are designed for processing sequential data with temporal dependencies, such as time series, text, and speech. RNNs have feedback connections that allow them to maintain a memory of past inputs and make decisions based on sequential information. Long Short-Term Memory (LSTM) and Gated Recurrent Unit (GRU) are popular variants of RNNs that address the vanishing gradient problem and capture long-term dependencies.

CLI command to create a recurrent neural network using Python with the TensorFlow library:

pythonCopy code

```
from tensorflow.keras.layers import LSTM # Define the recurrent neural network architecture model = Sequential([ LSTM(64, input_shape=(timesteps, input_dim)), Dense(num_classes, activation='softmax') ]) # Compile the model model.compile(optimizer='adam', loss='sparse_categorical_crossentropy', metrics=['accuracy']) # Train the model model.fit(train_sequences, train_labels, epochs=10, batch_size=32, validation_data=(val_sequences, val_labels))
```

This command will define a recurrent neural network model with an LSTM layer for sequence processing. The model will be compiled with the Adam optimizer and sparse categorical cross-entropy loss function and trained on the sequential data for a specified number of epochs and batch size.

In summary, neural network architectures such as feedforward, convolutional, and recurrent networks have revolutionized the field of machine learning and artificial intelligence by enabling the development of sophisticated models capable of handling complex data and tasks. By understanding the principles and applications of these architectures, practitioners can leverage their capabilities to solve diverse problems across domains.

Chapter 6: Ensemble Learning Approaches

Bagging and boosting are ensemble learning methods that aim to improve the predictive performance of machine learning models by combining multiple base learners. In this section, we will explore the principles behind bagging and boosting, their implementation using popular algorithms, and their applications across various domains.

Bagging (Bootstrap Aggregating): Bagging is a technique that involves training multiple independent models using random subsets of the training data and aggregating their predictions to make the final prediction. The key idea behind bagging is to reduce variance by averaging the predictions of diverse models trained on different subsets of the data. The most common algorithm for bagging is Random Forest, which constructs a collection of decision trees using bootstrapped samples of the training data and aggregates their predictions through voting or averaging.

CLI command to train a Random Forest model using Python with the scikit-learn library:

pythonCopy code

```
from sklearn.ensemble import RandomForestClassifier # Define the Random Forest classifier rf_classifier = RandomForestClassifier(n_estimators=100, max_depth=10, random_state=42) # Train the model rf_classifier.fit(train_data, train_labels) # Make predictions predictions = rf_classifier.predict(test_data)
```

This command will create a Random Forest classifier with 100 decision trees and a maximum depth of 10. It will then train the classifier on the labeled training data and use it to make predictions on the test data.

Boosting: Boosting is a sequential ensemble learning technique that trains a series of weak learners sequentially, with each subsequent learner focusing on the instances that were misclassified by the previous ones. Boosting aims to reduce bias by emphasizing the difficult-to-classify instances, thereby improving the overall predictive performance of the ensemble. One of the most popular boosting algorithms is Gradient Boosting Machines (GBM), which iteratively fits new models to the residuals of the previous models.

CLI command to train a Gradient Boosting model using Python with the XGBoost library:

pythonCopy code

```
import xgboost as xgb # Define the Gradient Boosting classifier                gbm_classifier             = xgb.XGBClassifier(n_estimators=100,    max_depth=3, learning_rate=0.1, random_state=42) # Train the model gbm_classifier.fit(train_data,    train_labels)   #   Make predictions                 predictions              = gbm_classifier.predict(test_data)
```

This command will create a Gradient Boosting classifier with 100 boosting rounds, a maximum depth of 3, and a learning rate of 0.1. It will then train the classifier on the labeled training data and use it to make predictions on the test data.

Applications: Bagging and boosting techniques are widely used in various machine learning tasks, including classification, regression, and anomaly detection. They have been successfully applied in domains such as finance, healthcare, e-commerce, and cybersecurity. For example, in finance, ensemble methods are used for credit scoring, fraud detection, and portfolio management, where accurate predictions are crucial for decision-making.

In summary, bagging and boosting are powerful ensemble learning techniques that can significantly improve the predictive performance of machine learning models. By combining multiple weak learners into a strong ensemble, these techniques can effectively mitigate bias and variance, leading to more robust and accurate predictions. Practitioners can leverage bagging and boosting algorithms such as Random Forest and Gradient Boosting Machines to tackle a wide range of real-world problems across different domains.

Ensemble methods have gained widespread popularity in the field of machine learning for both regression and classification tasks. They involve combining multiple base models to improve predictive accuracy and generalization performance. In this section, we will delve into the principles behind ensemble methods, explore various techniques for ensemble learning, and discuss their applications in both regression and classification scenarios.

Introduction to Ensemble Methods: Ensemble methods leverage the wisdom of crowds by aggregating predictions from multiple individual models to obtain a more robust and accurate prediction. The underlying idea is that by combining the predictions of diverse models, ensemble methods can mitigate the weaknesses of individual models and exploit their collective strengths. Ensemble methods can be broadly categorized into two main types: averaging-based methods and boosting-based methods.

CLI command to install the necessary Python libraries for ensemble learning:

bashCopy code

pip install scikit-learn xgboost

This command will install the scikit-learn library, which provides implementations of various ensemble techniques, and the XGBoost library, which is a popular gradient boosting framework.

Averaging-Based Ensemble Methods: Averaging-based ensemble methods, such as Bagging and Random Forest, involve training multiple independent models in parallel and averaging their predictions to make the final prediction. Bagging, short for Bootstrap Aggregating, constructs diverse models by training each model on a bootstrapped sample of the training data. Random Forest extends this idea by building a collection of decision trees and averaging their predictions.

CLI command to train a Random Forest classifier for classification using scikit-learn:

pythonCopy code

from sklearn.ensemble import RandomForestClassifier # Define the Random Forest classifier rf_classifier = RandomForestClassifier(n_estimators=100, max_depth=10, random_state=42) # Train the classifier rf_classifier.fit(X_train, y_train) # Make predictions predictions = rf_classifier.predict(X_test)

This command will create a Random Forest classifier with 100 decision trees, each with a maximum depth of 10. It will then train the classifier on the training data (X_train and y_train) and use it to make predictions on the test data (X_test).

Boosting-Based Ensemble Methods: Boosting-based ensemble methods, such as AdaBoost and Gradient Boosting Machines (GBM), sequentially train multiple weak learners, with each subsequent learner focusing on the mistakes made by the previous ones. AdaBoost assigns higher weights to misclassified instances, while GBM fits new models to the residuals of the previous models. These methods iteratively improve the ensemble's predictive performance by emphasizing difficult-to-predict instances.

CLI command to train an AdaBoost classifier for classification using scikit-learn:

pythonCopy code

```
from sklearn.ensemble import AdaBoostClassifier # Define the AdaBoost classifier adaboost_classifier = AdaBoostClassifier(n_estimators=100, learning_rate=1.0, random_state=42) # Train the classifier adaboost_classifier.fit(X_train, y_train) # Make predictions predictions = adaboost_classifier.predict(X_test)
```

This command will create an AdaBoost classifier with 100 weak learners and a learning rate of 1.0. It will then train the classifier on the training data (X_train and y_train) and use it to make predictions on the test data (X_test).

Applications of Ensemble Methods: Ensemble methods are widely used in various real-world applications, including credit scoring, fraud detection, image recognition, and recommendation systems. In credit scoring, ensemble methods can combine multiple predictive models to assess the creditworthiness of loan applicants more accurately. In fraud detection, ensemble methods can identify suspicious patterns by aggregating signals from different fraud detection algorithms.

In summary, ensemble methods are powerful techniques for improving predictive accuracy and generalization performance in both regression and classification tasks. By combining the predictions of diverse models, ensemble methods can overcome the limitations of individual models and achieve superior performance. Practitioners can leverage ensemble methods such as Bagging, Random Forest, AdaBoost, and Gradient Boosting Machines to tackle a wide range of machine learning problems across various domains.

Chapter 7: Dimensionality Reduction Techniques

Principal Component Analysis (PCA) is a widely used dimensionality reduction technique that extracts the most important features from high-dimensional data while preserving the variance in the data as much as possible. In this section, we will delve into the principles behind PCA, discuss its mathematical formulation, explore its applications in various domains, and provide practical examples of deploying PCA using Python.

Introduction to Principal Component Analysis: Principal Component Analysis (PCA) is a statistical method used to reduce the dimensionality of high-dimensional data while retaining most of the original information. The key idea behind PCA is to transform the data into a new coordinate system, called the principal components, where the data variance is maximized along the axes.

CLI command to install the necessary Python library for PCA:

bashCopy code

```
pip install scikit-learn
```

This command will install the scikit-learn library, which provides implementations of various machine learning algorithms, including PCA.

Mathematical Formulation of PCA: PCA aims to find a set of orthogonal vectors, known as principal components, that capture the maximum variance in the data. Given a dataset with m observations and n features, PCA constructs a covariance matrix Σ and computes its eigenvectors and eigenvalues. The eigenvectors represent the directions of maximum variance, while the eigenvalues indicate the amount of variance explained by each principal component.

CLI command to perform PCA using scikit-learn in Python:

pythonCopy code

```
from sklearn.decomposition import PCA # Define the
PCA transformer pca = PCA(n_components=2) # Fit PCA
to the data and transform it X_pca =
pca.fit_transform(X)
```

This command will create a PCA transformer with two principal components and fit it to the data matrix ◆X. It will then transform the data into the new principal component space.

Applications of PCA: PCA has various applications across different domains, including data compression, visualization, and feature extraction. In data compression, PCA reduces the dimensionality of large datasets while preserving most of the important information, making it easier to store and analyze the data. In visualization, PCA can be used to project high-dimensional data onto a lower-dimensional space for visualization purposes, allowing analysts to explore the underlying structure of the data more effectively. In feature extraction, PCA can help identify the most important features in the data, facilitating subsequent machine learning tasks.

Practical Example: PCA for Dimensionality Reduction: Suppose we have a dataset containing images of handwritten digits, each represented as a vector of pixel values. We can use PCA to reduce the dimensionality of the data and visualize the digits in a lower-dimensional space.

CLI command to perform PCA for dimensionality reduction in Python:

pythonCopy code

```
from sklearn.datasets import load_digits import matplotlib.pyplot as plt # Load the digits dataset digits = load_digits() X = digits.data y = digits.target # Perform PCA for dimensionality reduction pca = PCA(n_components=2) X_pca = pca.fit_transform(X) # Plot the transformed data plt.figure(figsize=(8, 6)) plt.scatter(X_pca[:, 0], X_pca[:, 1], c=y, cmap='viridis') plt.title('PCA for Dimensionality Reduction') plt.xlabel('Principal Component 1') plt.ylabel('Principal Component 2') plt.colorbar(label='Digit Label') plt.show()
```

This command will load the digits dataset, perform PCA for dimensionality reduction, and visualize the transformed data in a two-dimensional space.

In summary, Principal Component Analysis (PCA) is a powerful technique for dimensionality reduction, data compression, and feature extraction. By transforming high-dimensional data into a lower-dimensional space while preserving most of the variance, PCA enables efficient data analysis, visualization, and interpretation. Practitioners can leverage PCA to preprocess data, visualize complex datasets, and improve the performance of machine learning models across various domains.

t-Distributed Stochastic Neighbor Embedding (t-SNE) is a powerful nonlinear dimensionality reduction technique used for visualizing high-dimensional data in a low-dimensional space. In this section, we will explore the principles behind t-SNE, discuss its advantages and limitations, demonstrate how to deploy the technique using Python, and provide practical examples of its applications in various domains.

Introduction to t-Distributed Stochastic Neighbor Embedding: t-Distributed Stochastic Neighbor Embedding (t-SNE) is a dimensionality reduction technique that maps high-dimensional data points to a low-dimensional space, typically two or three dimensions, while preserving the local structure of the data as much as possible. Unlike linear methods such as PCA, t-SNE focuses on preserving the pairwise similarities between data points in the lower-dimensional space.

CLI command to install the necessary Python library for t-SNE:

bashCopy code

```
pip install scikit-learn
```

This command will install the scikit-learn library, which provides implementations of various machine learning algorithms, including t-SNE.

How t-SNE Works: t-SNE works by first computing pairwise similarities between data points in the high-dimensional space using a Gaussian kernel. It then constructs a probability distribution over pairs of data points in both the high-dimensional and low-dimensional spaces. Next, it minimizes the Kullback-Leibler divergence between the two probability distributions, effectively preserving the local structure of the data in the lower-dimensional space.

CLI command to perform t-SNE visualization using scikit-learn in Python:

pythonCopy code

```
from sklearn.manifold import TSNE # Define the t-SNE transformer tsne = TSNE(n_components=2, perplexity=30, learning_rate=200) # Fit t-SNE to the data and transform it X_tsne = tsne.fit_transform(X)
```

This command will create a t-SNE transformer with two dimensions, a perplexity of 30, and a learning rate of 200. It will then fit the transformer to the data matrix ◆X and transform the data into the lower-dimensional t-SNE space.

Advantages and Limitations of t-SNE: One of the main advantages of t-SNE is its ability to reveal the underlying structure of complex datasets by preserving the local relationships between data points. It is particularly effective for visualizing clusters and identifying patterns in high-dimensional data. However, t-SNE has some limitations, such as its sensitivity to the choice of hyperparameters and its computational complexity, which can make it impractical for large datasets.

Practical Example: Visualizing High-Dimensional Data with t-SNE: Suppose we have a dataset containing images of handwritten digits, each represented as a vector of pixel values. We can use t-SNE to visualize the high-dimensional data in a two-dimensional space while preserving the local structure of the digits.

CLI command to perform t-SNE visualization for image data in Python:

pythonCopy code

```
from sklearn.datasets import load_digits import
matplotlib.pyplot as plt # Load the digits dataset digits =
load_digits() X = digits.data y = digits.target # Perform t-
SNE for visualization tsne = TSNE(n_components=2,
perplexity=30, learning_rate=200) X_tsne =
tsne.fit_transform(X) # Plot the transformed data
plt.figure(figsize=(8, 6)) plt.scatter(X_tsne[:, 0], X_tsne[:,
1], c=y, cmap='viridis') plt.title('t-SNE Visualization of
Handwritten Digits') plt.xlabel('t-SNE Component 1')
plt.ylabel('t-SNE Component 2') plt.colorbar(label='Digit
Label') plt.show()
```

This command will load the digits dataset, perform t-SNE for visualization, and plot the transformed data in a two-dimensional space.

In summary, t-Distributed Stochastic Neighbor Embedding (t-SNE) is a valuable tool for visualizing high-dimensional data in a low-dimensional space while preserving local relationships between data points. Despite its limitations, t-SNE can provide insights into the structure and patterns present in complex datasets, making it an essential technique in data analysis and visualization. Practitioners can leverage t-SNE to explore and understand high-dimensional data across various domains, including image analysis, genomics, and natural language processing.

Chapter 8: Time Series Analysis and Forecasting

Time series data refers to a sequence of observations recorded at regular time intervals. It is commonly encountered in various fields such as finance, economics, weather forecasting, and signal processing. In this section, we will explore the characteristics of time series data, discuss its components, and demonstrate how to analyze and visualize time series data using Python libraries such as Pandas and Matplotlib.

Understanding Time Series Data: Time series data consists of observations collected over successive time periods, such as days, months, or years. Each observation is associated with a specific time stamp, allowing analysts to track changes in the data over time. Time series data often exhibits patterns, trends, seasonality, and irregular fluctuations, which can be analyzed to uncover underlying relationships and make predictions.

CLI command to install the necessary Python libraries for time series analysis:

bashCopy code

pip install pandas matplotlib

This command will install the Pandas library for data manipulation and the Matplotlib library for data visualization, both of which are commonly used for analyzing time series data in Python.

Components of Time Series Data: Time series data can be decomposed into several components, each of which represents a different aspect of the data's behavior:

Trend: The long-term movement or directionality of the data, indicating whether the data is increasing, decreasing, or stable over time.

Seasonality: Patterns or fluctuations that occur at regular intervals, such as daily, weekly, or yearly cycles.

Cyclical Variations: Non-periodic fluctuations in the data that occur over longer time periods, often associated with economic cycles or business cycles.

Irregular or Residual: Random fluctuations or noise in the data that cannot be attributed to the trend, seasonality, or cyclical variations.

Analyzing Time Series Data with Python: We can use Python libraries such as Pandas and Matplotlib to analyze and visualize time series data effectively. First, we need to load the time series data into a Pandas DataFrame and convert the date column to a datetime format for time-based indexing.

CLI command to load time series data into a Pandas DataFrame in Python:

pythonCopy code

```
import pandas as pd # Load time series data from a CSV file df = pd.read_csv('time_series_data.csv') # Convert the date column to datetime format df['Date'] = pd.to_datetime(df['Date']) # Set the date
```

column as the index df.set_index('Date', inplace=True)

This command will load the time series data from a CSV file into a Pandas DataFrame, convert the date column to datetime format, and set it as the index for time-based indexing.

Visualizing Time Series Data: Once we have loaded the time series data into a Pandas DataFrame, we can use Matplotlib to visualize the data, including its trend, seasonality, and other components.

CLI command to plot time series data using Matplotlib in Python:

pythonCopy code

```
import matplotlib.pyplot as plt # Plot the time series data plt.figure(figsize=(10, 6)) plt.plot(df.index, df['Value'], color='blue', linewidth=1) plt.title('Time Series Data Visualization') plt.xlabel('Date') plt.ylabel('Value') plt.grid(True) plt.show()
```

This command will plot the time series data using Matplotlib, with the date on the x-axis and the corresponding values on the y-axis.

In summary, time series data is a fundamental type of data that represents observations collected over successive time periods. By understanding the components of time series data and using appropriate analysis and visualization techniques, analysts can uncover insights, identify patterns, and make informed decisions in various domains. Python libraries such as Pandas and Matplotlib provide powerful tools for analyzing and visualizing time series data, making it accessible to analysts and data scientists for exploratory data analysis and forecasting tasks.

Forecasting is a crucial aspect of decision-making in many fields, ranging from finance and economics to weather forecasting and supply chain management. It involves predicting future values or trends based on historical data and other relevant factors. In this section, we will explore various forecasting methods and models, including time series forecasting, machine learning approaches, and statistical techniques, and discuss how they can be applied to different domains.

Introduction to Forecasting: Forecasting is the process of making predictions about future events or outcomes based on past and present data. It plays a vital role in planning, budgeting, resource allocation, and risk management in organizations. Forecasting techniques aim to capture patterns, trends, and relationships in the data to make accurate predictions about future values or trends.

CLI command to install the necessary Python libraries for forecasting:

bashCopy code

```
pip install statsmodels scikit-learn
```

This command will install the Statsmodels library for time series analysis and the Scikit-learn library for machine learning algorithms, both of which are commonly used for forecasting in Python.

Time Series Forecasting: Time series forecasting is a popular approach for predicting future values based on historical data. It involves analyzing the temporal patterns and trends in the data and using them to make projections about future values. Time series forecasting models include autoregressive integrated moving average (ARIMA), seasonal decomposition of time series (STL), exponential smoothing methods, and Fourier analysis.

CLI command to fit an ARIMA model to time series data using Python:

pythonCopy code

```
from statsmodels.tsa.arima.model import ARIMA # Fit an ARIMA model to the time series data model = ARIMA(data, order=(p, d, q)) result = model.fit()
```

This command will fit an ARIMA model to the time series data, where p, d, and q are the parameters representing the autoregressive, differencing, and moving average components of the model, respectively.

Machine Learning for Forecasting: Machine learning techniques offer powerful tools for forecasting by learning patterns and relationships from data and making predictions based on learned patterns. Supervised learning algorithms such as regression, support vector machines (SVM), and random forests can be applied to time series data to predict future values. Additionally, neural networks, including recurrent neural networks (RNNs) and long short-term memory (LSTM) networks, have shown promising results in time series forecasting tasks.

CLI command to train a random forest regressor for time series forecasting in Python:

pythonCopy code

```
from sklearn.ensemble import RandomForestRegressor # Train a random forest regressor model model = RandomForestRegressor(n_estimators=100)
model.fit(X_train, y_train)
```

This command will train a random forest regressor model using the RandomForestRegressor class from the Scikit-learn library, with 100 decision trees (n_estimators) in the ensemble.

Statistical Forecasting Techniques: Statistical forecasting techniques use mathematical models and statistical methods to analyze historical data and make predictions about future values. These techniques include simple moving averages, exponential smoothing, trend analysis, and regression analysis. They are particularly useful for short-term forecasting and for capturing seasonality and trend patterns in the data.

CLI command to calculate a simple moving average for time series forecasting in Python:

pythonCopy code

```
# Calculate a simple moving average moving_avg = data.rolling(window=12).mean()
```

This command will calculate a simple moving average for the time series data using a window size of 12 months, which smooths out short-term fluctuations and highlights longer-term trends.

In summary, forecasting methods and models play a crucial role in predicting future values and trends based on historical data. Time series forecasting techniques, machine learning approaches, and statistical methods offer various tools and algorithms for making accurate predictions in different domains. By understanding the principles and applications of forecasting, analysts and decision-makers can leverage these techniques to anticipate future outcomes, mitigate risks, and optimize resource allocation in their organizations.

Chapter 9: Reinforcement Learning in Big Data

Reinforcement learning (RL) is a branch of machine learning concerned with how software agents ought to take actions in an environment to maximize some notion of cumulative reward. It's a type of learning that enables an agent to learn through trial and error by interacting with its environment. In this section, we'll delve into the fundamental concepts of reinforcement learning, explore its key components, discuss different types of reinforcement learning algorithms, and highlight its applications across various domains.

Understanding Reinforcement Learning: Reinforcement learning is inspired by behavioral psychology, where an agent learns to make decisions through interaction with an environment to achieve a specific goal. Unlike supervised learning, where the algorithm is trained on labeled data, and unsupervised learning, where the algorithm discovers patterns in unlabeled data, reinforcement learning is based on learning from feedback received from the environment. The agent takes actions, receives feedback in the form of rewards or penalties, and adjusts its strategy to maximize cumulative rewards over time.

CLI command to install reinforcement learning libraries in Python:

bashCopy code

pip install gym tensorflow keras

This command will install the Gym library, an open-source toolkit for developing and comparing reinforcement learning algorithms, and the TensorFlow and Keras libraries, which are commonly used for building and training neural networks in Python.

Key Components of Reinforcement Learning: Reinforcement learning involves several key components, including:

Agent: The entity that learns and makes decisions in the environment.

Environment: The external system with which the agent interacts.

State: A representation of the environment at a particular time step.

Action: The decision or choice made by the agent to transition from one state to another.

Reward: A scalar feedback signal received by the agent after taking an action, indicating the desirability of the action.

Together, these components form the basis of the reinforcement learning framework, where the agent learns to take actions that maximize the cumulative reward over time.

Types of Reinforcement Learning Algorithms: There are several types of reinforcement learning algorithms, including:

Value-Based Methods: Algorithms that learn to estimate the value of being in a particular state or taking a particular action.

Policy-Based Methods: Algorithms that directly learn the optimal policy, i.e., the mapping from states to actions.

Model-Based Methods: Algorithms that learn a model of the environment dynamics and use it to plan future actions.

Examples of popular reinforcement learning algorithms include Q-learning, Deep Q-Networks (DQN), Policy Gradient methods, and Actor-Critic methods.

CLI command to train a Q-learning agent using Gym in Python:

pythonCopy code

```
import gym import numpy as np # Create the environment env = gym.make('CartPole-v1') # Initialize the Q-table Q = np.zeros([env.observation_space.n, env.action_space.n]) # Set hyperparameters alpha = 0.1 # Learning rate gamma = 0.9 # Discount factor epsilon = 0.1 # Exploration rate # Train the agent for episode in range(1, 1001): state = env.reset() done = False while not done: if np.random.rand() < epsilon: action = env.action_space.sample() # Explore else: action = np.argmax(Q[state]) # Exploit next_state, reward, done, _ = env.step(action) Q[state, action] += alpha * (reward + gamma * np.max(Q[next_state]) - Q[state, action]) state = next_state # Evaluate the
```

```
trained agent total_rewards = [] for episode in
range(100): state = env.reset() done = False
total_reward = 0 while not done: action =
np.argmax(Q[state]) state, reward, done, _ =
env.step(action) total_reward += reward
total_rewards.append(total_reward) average_reward
= np.mean(total_rewards) print("Average reward:",
average_reward)
```

This Python code trains a Q-learning agent to solve the CartPole environment in OpenAI Gym. It initializes the Q-table, explores and exploits actions, updates the Q-values based on rewards, and evaluates the trained agent's performance.

Applications of Reinforcement Learning: Reinforcement learning has numerous applications across various domains, including:

Robotics: Reinforcement learning can be used to train robots to perform complex tasks such as object manipulation, navigation, and autonomous driving.

Gaming: Reinforcement learning algorithms have been successfully applied to develop agents that play video games at human or superhuman levels.

Finance: Reinforcement learning can be used to optimize trading strategies, portfolio management, and risk assessment in financial markets.

Healthcare: Reinforcement learning techniques can assist in personalized treatment planning, medical diagnosis, and drug discovery.

Overall, reinforcement learning is a powerful paradigm for learning to make decisions in complex, uncertain environments. By understanding its principles, algorithms, and applications, researchers and practitioners can leverage reinforcement learning to solve a wide range of real-world problems and advance the field of artificial intelligence.

Reinforcement learning (RL) is a powerful machine learning technique that has found numerous applications in various domains, including big data analytics. In this section, we will explore how reinforcement learning techniques can be applied to tackle challenges in big data processing, analysis, and optimization. We will discuss specific use cases and scenarios where reinforcement learning algorithms offer unique advantages and opportunities for innovation.

Dynamic Resource Allocation: One of the key challenges in big data processing is dynamically allocating computational resources to optimize performance and minimize costs. Traditional approaches often rely on static resource allocation strategies, which may not adapt well to changing workloads and resource demands. Reinforcement learning algorithms can learn to dynamically allocate resources based on current system conditions and workload characteristics, leading to improved efficiency and resource utilization.

CLI command to deploy a reinforcement learning-based resource allocation system:

bashCopy code

```
kubectl apply -f rl-resource-allocation.yaml
```

This command deploys a Kubernetes application that uses reinforcement learning to allocate resources dynamically across a cluster of servers based on real-time workload metrics.

Automated Data Cleansing and Preprocessing: Data cleansing and preprocessing are essential steps in the data analysis pipeline, but they can be time-consuming and labor-intensive, especially for large-scale datasets. Reinforcement learning techniques can automate the data cleansing process by learning to identify and correct errors, outliers, and missing values in the data. By continuously learning from feedback and improving over time, RL-based data cleansing systems can handle diverse data formats and quality issues more effectively than traditional rule-based approaches.

CLI command to train a reinforcement learning agent for data cleansing:

pythonCopy code

```
python train_rl_agent.py --dataset=data.csv --epochs=1000
```

This command trains a reinforcement learning agent using the specified dataset and conducts multiple epochs of training to optimize the agent's performance in data cleansing tasks.

Adaptive Query Optimization: Query optimization is a critical aspect of database management systems, particularly in the context of big data analytics, where queries may involve complex joins, aggregations, and transformations on large datasets. Reinforcement learning algorithms can be used to learn query optimization strategies based on past query execution times, resource usage, and query plans. By learning from historical data and feedback from query executions, RL-based query optimizers can adaptively adjust query plans to improve performance and efficiency.

CLI command to deploy a reinforcement learning-based query optimizer:

bashCopy code

```
docker run -d --name rl-query-optimizer rl-query-optimizer:latest
```

This command deploys a Docker container running a reinforcement learning-based query optimizer that continuously learns and improves query execution plans based on real-time feedback from query executions.

Anomaly Detection and Predictive Maintenance: Detecting anomalies and identifying potential failures in big data systems is crucial for ensuring reliability, availability, and performance. Reinforcement learning algorithms can be trained to detect anomalies in system logs, sensor data, and operational metrics by learning normal patterns and behaviors. RL-based anomaly detection systems can adapt to changes in system behavior and identify emerging issues before they escalate into major problems, enabling proactive maintenance and troubleshooting.

CLI command to train a reinforcement learning agent for anomaly detection:

```
pythonCopy code
python        train_rl_anomaly_detector.py        --
dataset=logs.csv --epochs=1000
```

This command trains a reinforcement learning agent using the specified log dataset and conducts multiple epochs of training to detect anomalies and abnormal patterns in the data.

In summary, reinforcement learning offers promising opportunities for addressing various challenges in big data analytics, including resource allocation, data cleansing, query optimization, and anomaly detection. By leveraging RL techniques, organizations can build intelligent systems that continuously learn and adapt to evolving data and workload conditions, leading to improved efficiency, reliability, and performance in big data environments.

Chapter 10: Advanced Applications of Machine Learning in Big Data Analysis

Predictive maintenance is a proactive approach to maintenance that aims to predict when equipment or machinery is likely to fail so that maintenance can be performed just in time to prevent costly downtime and repairs. In recent years, machine learning techniques have emerged as powerful tools for predictive maintenance, enabling organizations to analyze vast amounts of sensor data, historical maintenance records, and operational data to predict equipment failures with high accuracy. In this section, we will explore the applications of machine learning for predictive maintenance, discuss common algorithms and techniques used, and examine real-world use cases and deployments.

Introduction to Predictive Maintenance: Predictive maintenance involves leveraging data-driven insights to anticipate equipment failures and schedule maintenance activities accordingly. Traditional approaches to maintenance, such as reactive and preventive maintenance, are often inefficient and costly, as they either wait for equipment to fail before taking action or perform maintenance tasks on a fixed schedule regardless of the actual condition of the equipment. Predictive maintenance, on the other hand, relies on predictive models built using machine learning algorithms to forecast when equipment failure is likely to occur based on historical data and real-time sensor readings.

CLI command to install Python libraries for predictive maintenance:

bashCopy code

```
pip install numpy pandas scikit-learn matplotlib seaborn
```

This command installs the necessary Python libraries, including NumPy, pandas, scikit-learn, matplotlib, and seaborn, for data preprocessing, modeling, and visualization in predictive maintenance projects.

Data Collection and Preprocessing: A crucial step in implementing predictive maintenance is collecting and preprocessing the relevant data. This typically involves gathering sensor data from equipment, historical maintenance records, and contextual data such as operating conditions and environmental factors. The collected data may be in various formats and may contain missing values, outliers, and noise that need to be addressed before training machine learning models. Data preprocessing techniques such as cleaning, normalization, feature engineering, and dimensionality reduction are used to prepare the data for modeling.

CLI command to collect sensor data from equipment:

bashCopy code

```
python collect_sensor_data.py --equipment_id=123 --duration=30 --output=data.csv
```

This command collects sensor data from equipment with the specified ID for a duration of 30 days and saves the data to a CSV file for further analysis and preprocessing.

Feature Engineering and Selection: Feature engineering plays a crucial role in predictive maintenance by extracting relevant features from raw sensor data and historical records to represent the health and condition of the equipment. Features may include statistical metrics, time-series aggregates, frequency domain features, and domain-specific indicators of degradation or failure. Feature selection techniques such as correlation analysis, mutual information, and model-based selection are used to identify the most informative features for training predictive models.

CLI command to perform feature engineering and selection:

bashCopy code

```
python feature_engineering.py --input=data.csv --output=features.csv
```

This command processes the raw sensor data and historical records stored in the input CSV file, performs feature engineering to extract relevant features, and selects the most informative features for predictive modeling, saving the processed data to a new CSV file.

Modeling and Prediction: Once the data has been collected, preprocessed, and engineered, machine learning models can be trained to predict equipment failures. Common algorithms used for predictive maintenance include supervised learning algorithms such as logistic regression, random forests, support vector machines, and deep learning models such as recurrent neural networks (RNNs) and long short-term memory networks (LSTMs). These models are trained on historical data with labeled failure events to learn patterns and relationships between sensor readings and impending failures.

CLI command to train a predictive maintenance model:

bashCopy code

```
python train_predictive_model.py --input=features.csv --model=random_forest --output=model.pkl
```

This command trains a predictive maintenance model using the features extracted from the preprocessed data stored in the input CSV file. The model is trained using the specified algorithm (e.g., random forest) and saved to a file for future use in making predictions.

Deployment and Monitoring: Once the predictive maintenance model has been trained, it can be deployed in production environments to monitor equipment health and predict failures in real-time. The model continuously analyzes incoming sensor data, generates predictions of future failures, and triggers maintenance alerts when anomalies or degradation patterns are detected. Monitoring the performance of the deployed model is essential to ensure that it remains accurate and effective over time, and periodic model retraining may be necessary to adapt to changing operating conditions and data distributions.

CLI command to deploy a predictive maintenance model:

bashCopy code

```
python          deploy_predictive_model.py      --
model=model.pkl          --threshold=0.5          --
alert_system=slack
```

This command deploys the trained predictive maintenance model stored in the model file and sets a threshold for triggering maintenance alerts. When the model predicts a failure probability above the threshold, an alert is sent to the specified alert system (e.g., Slack) to notify maintenance personnel to take action.

In summary, machine learning techniques have revolutionized predictive maintenance by enabling organizations to predict equipment failures with greater accuracy and efficiency. By leveraging data-driven insights and advanced algorithms, predictive maintenance systems can reduce downtime, improve operational efficiency, and extend the lifespan of critical assets, leading to significant cost savings and operational improvements for businesses across various industries.

Personalized recommendations have become an integral part of our daily lives, shaping our online experiences by providing tailored suggestions for products, services, content, and more. Machine learning lies at the heart of personalized recommendation systems, enabling businesses to analyze user preferences, behaviors, and interactions to deliver relevant and engaging recommendations. In this section, we will explore the role of machine learning in personalized recommendations, discuss common algorithms and techniques used, and examine real-world applications and deployments.

Introduction to Personalized Recommendations: Personalized recommendations aim to enhance user engagement and satisfaction by delivering relevant and timely suggestions based on individual preferences and interests. Traditional approaches to recommendations, such as rule-based systems and manual curation, are limited in their ability to scale and adapt to diverse user preferences and changing contexts. Machine learning-based recommendation systems leverage algorithms and models to analyze large volumes of user data, identify patterns and similarities, and generate personalized recommendations that maximize user satisfaction and engagement.

CLI command to install Python libraries for recommendation systems:

bashCopy code

```
pip install numpy pandas scikit-learn tensorflow
```

This command installs the necessary Python libraries, including NumPy, pandas, scikit-learn, and TensorFlow, for building and training recommendation models.

Collaborative Filtering: Collaborative filtering is a popular technique used in personalized recommendation systems to generate recommendations based on user interactions and feedback. The fundamental idea behind collaborative filtering is to identify similarities between users or items and recommend items that similar users have liked or interacted with in the past. There are two main approaches to collaborative filtering: user-based and item-based. User-based collaborative filtering recommends items to a user based on the preferences of similar users, while item-based collaborative filtering recommends items similar to those the user has previously liked or interacted with.

CLI command to train a collaborative filtering model:

bashCopy code

```
python train_collaborative_filtering.py --input=interactions.csv --model=user_based --output=model.pkl
```

This command trains a collaborative filtering model using the user interactions stored in the input CSV file and saves the trained model to a file for making recommendations.

Content-Based Filtering: Content-based filtering is another common approach to personalized recommendations that leverages the attributes or features of items to generate recommendations. In content-based filtering, items are represented as feature vectors, and recommendations are made based on the similarity between the features of items and the user's preferences or profile. Content-based filtering is particularly useful in scenarios where user-item interactions are sparse or unavailable, as it relies solely on item attributes to make recommendations.

CLI command to train a content-based filtering model:
bashCopy code

```
python        train_content_based_filtering.py        --input=items.csv --model=tfidf --output=model.pkl
```

This command trains a content-based filtering model using the attributes of items stored in the input CSV file and saves the trained model to a file for making recommendations.

Hybrid Recommendation Systems: Hybrid recommendation systems combine multiple recommendation techniques, such as collaborative filtering, content-based filtering, and contextual information, to generate more accurate and diverse recommendations. By leveraging the strengths of different recommendation approaches, hybrid systems can overcome the limitations of individual methods and provide more personalized and relevant recommendations to users. Hybrid recommendation systems are widely used in e-commerce, streaming platforms, and content aggregation services to deliver a superior recommendation experience to users.

CLI command to deploy a hybrid recommendation system:
bashCopy code

```
python deploy_hybrid_recommendation_system.py --
models=model1.pkl model2.pkl --weights=0.7 0.3 --
output=model.pkl
```

This command deploys a hybrid recommendation system that combines two trained recommendation models stored in the specified model files. The weights parameter specifies the relative importance of each model in generating recommendations, and the output parameter specifies the file to save the deployed model.

In summary, machine learning plays a crucial role in personalized recommendation systems, enabling businesses to deliver relevant and engaging recommendations to users based on their preferences and behaviors. By leveraging collaborative filtering, content-based filtering, and hybrid approaches, recommendation systems can provide personalized experiences across a wide range of domains, including e-commerce, media, entertainment, and social networking, ultimately driving user engagement, satisfaction, and loyalty.

BOOK 4
BIG DATA ARCHITECTURE AND SCALABILITY:
DESIGNING ROBUST SYSTEMS FOR ENTERPRISE
SOLUTIONS

ROB BOTWRIGHT

Chapter 1: Introduction to Big Data Architecture

In the realm of big data, architecture plays a pivotal role in designing robust, scalable, and efficient systems for processing, storing, and analyzing vast amounts of data. Big data architecture encompasses a wide array of components, each serving a specific function in the data lifecycle, from ingestion to insights generation. In this section, we will delve into the key components of big data architecture, explore their functionalities, and discuss best practices for deploying and managing these components effectively.

Distributed File Systems: At the core of many big data architectures lie distributed file systems, which provide a scalable and fault-tolerant storage solution for massive datasets. Examples of popular distributed file systems include Hadoop Distributed File System (HDFS), Amazon Simple Storage Service (S3), and Google Cloud Storage (GCS). These file systems divide data into blocks and distribute them across multiple nodes in a cluster, enabling parallel processing and high availability.

CLI command to set up a Hadoop Distributed File System:

bashCopy code

```
hadoop fs -mkdir /user/input
```

This command creates a directory named 'input' in the Hadoop file system.

Data Ingestion Frameworks: Data ingestion frameworks facilitate the seamless collection and ingestion of data from various sources into the big data platform. Apache Kafka, Apache NiFi, and AWS Kinesis are popular examples of data ingestion frameworks that support real-time data streaming and batch processing. These frameworks provide connectors and APIs for integrating with diverse data sources, such as databases, logs, sensors, and applications, enabling organizations to ingest data at scale.

CLI command to start Apache Kafka:

bashCopy code

```
bin/kafka-server-start.sh config/server.properties
```

This command starts the Kafka server using the configuration specified in the 'server.properties' file.

Batch Processing Engines: Batch processing engines are essential components of big data architectures for executing complex data processing tasks on large datasets. Apache Hadoop MapReduce and Apache Spark are widely used batch processing frameworks that support distributed computing and fault tolerance. These engines enable organizations to perform data transformations, aggregations, and analytics at scale, leveraging parallel processing across clusters of commodity hardware.

CLI command to submit a MapReduce job:

bashCopy code

```
hadoop jar <path-to-jar-file> <main-class> <input-path> <output-path>
```

This command submits a MapReduce job to the Hadoop cluster, specifying the input and output paths for processing.

Stream Processing Platforms: In addition to batch processing, many big data architectures incorporate stream processing platforms for real-time data processing and analysis. Stream processing platforms, such as Apache Flink, Apache Storm, and AWS Kinesis Data Streams, enable organizations to process and analyze continuous streams of data in near real-time, making timely decisions and extracting valuable insights from streaming data sources.

CLI command to deploy an Apache Flink job:

bashCopy code

```
flink run -c <main-class> <path-to-jar-file>
```

This command deploys a Flink job to the cluster, specifying the main class and the location of the JAR file containing the job code.

Data Storage Solutions: Data storage is a critical aspect of big data architecture, and organizations have a plethora of options for storing and managing diverse types of data. In addition to distributed file systems, organizations leverage NoSQL databases, such as Apache Cassandra, MongoDB, and Amazon DynamoDB, for storing structured and semi-structured data, and data warehouses, such as Google BigQuery and Amazon Redshift, for storing and querying structured data at scale.

CLI command to create a table in Apache Cassandra:

bashCopy code

```
cqlsh  -e  "CREATE  TABLE  <keyspace>.<table>
(<columns>) WITH <options>"
```
This command creates a table in the specified keyspace with the specified columns and options using the Cassandra Query Language (CQL).

Data Processing Frameworks: Data processing frameworks, such as Apache Beam and Apache Flink, provide high-level abstractions and APIs for building data processing pipelines that can handle both batch and stream processing workloads. These frameworks offer support for parallel execution, fault tolerance, and state management, enabling organizations to develop complex data processing workflows with ease.

CLI command to execute an Apache Beam pipeline:
bashCopy code

```
mvn  compile  exec:java  -Dexec.mainClass=<main-class> -Dexec.args="<arguments>"
```

This command compiles and executes an Apache Beam pipeline, specifying the main class and any additional arguments required for execution.

Data Governance and Security Tools: As organizations collect and process increasingly large volumes of data, ensuring data governance and security becomes paramount. Data governance and security tools, such as Apache Ranger, Apache Sentry, and AWS Identity and Access Management (IAM), help organizations enforce access controls, monitor data access and usage, and ensure compliance with regulatory requirements.

CLI command to configure Apache Ranger policies:
bashCopy code
ranger-admin start

This command starts the Apache Ranger Admin service, allowing administrators to configure and manage access policies for data resources.

In summary, big data architecture comprises a diverse set of components and technologies that collectively enable organizations to harness the power of data for insights and innovation. By understanding the functionalities and deployment considerations of these components, organizations can design and implement robust big data architectures that meet their specific requirements and objectives.

The evolution of big data architectures has been marked by significant advancements in technology, driven by the ever-increasing volume, velocity, and variety of data generated by modern organizations. Over the years, several key trends have emerged, shaping the development and adoption of big data architectures across industries. Next, we will explore the historical evolution of big data architectures, from early relational databases to modern distributed computing frameworks, and analyze current trends that are shaping the future of big data architecture.

Early Relational Databases: The journey of big data architectures can be traced back to the era of early relational databases, such as Oracle, IBM DB2, and Microsoft SQL Server. These databases were designed to store and manage structured data in a tabular format, offering features like ACID transactions, SQL querying, and data integrity constraints. While relational databases were sufficient for handling moderate-sized datasets, they struggled to cope with the massive volumes of data generated by internet-scale applications and platforms.

CLI command to create a table in Oracle Database:

bashCopy code

```
CREATE TABLE <table_name> ( <column1> <data_type>, <column2> <data_type>, ... );
```

This command creates a table in Oracle Database with the specified columns and data types.

Emergence of NoSQL Databases: The limitations of relational databases paved the way for the emergence of NoSQL (Not Only SQL) databases, which offered a more flexible and scalable approach to data storage and management. NoSQL databases, such as MongoDB, Cassandra, and Couchbase, embraced a schema-less data model, enabling organizations to store and process semi-structured and unstructured data with ease. These databases also introduced concepts like eventual consistency and horizontal scalability, allowing for distributed data storage and processing.

CLI command to insert data into a MongoDB collection:

bashCopy code

```
db.<collection_name>.insertOne({ <key1>: <value1>, <key2>: <value2>, ... });
```

This command inserts a document into a MongoDB collection with the specified fields and values.

Rise of Distributed Computing Frameworks: As the volume and variety of data continued to grow exponentially, traditional database systems struggled to keep pace with the demands of modern data-intensive applications. This led to the rise of distributed computing frameworks, such as Apache Hadoop and Apache Spark, which revolutionized the way large-scale data processing and analysis were performed. These frameworks introduced concepts like MapReduce and in-memory processing, enabling organizations to process massive datasets across clusters of commodity hardware in a fault-tolerant manner.

CLI command to submit a Spark job:

bashCopy code

```
spark-submit --class <main_class> --master <master_url> <path_to_jar> <arguments>
```

This command submits a Spark job to the cluster, specifying the main class, master URL, JAR file path, and any additional arguments required for execution.

Convergence of Batch and Stream Processing: With the proliferation of real-time data sources, there emerged a need for architectures that could handle both batch and stream processing workloads seamlessly. This led to the convergence of batch and stream processing frameworks, giving rise to platforms like Apache Flink and Apache Beam. These unified frameworks provided a common API for building and executing data processing pipelines that could handle both batch and stream data in a consistent and efficient manner, simplifying the development and deployment of real-time analytics applications.

CLI command to deploy an Apache Flink job:

bashCopy code

```
flink run -c <main_class> <path_to_jar>
```

This command deploys a Flink job to the cluster, specifying the main class and the location of the JAR file containing the job code.

Adoption of Cloud-Native Architectures: In recent years, there has been a significant shift towards cloud-native architectures, driven by the scalability, agility, and cost-effectiveness offered by cloud computing platforms like AWS, Azure, and Google Cloud. Cloud-native architectures leverage containerization, microservices, and serverless computing to build highly scalable and resilient data processing systems that can dynamically scale based on demand. This trend has democratized access to big data technologies, enabling organizations of all sizes to harness the power of data for insights and innovation.

CLI command to deploy a Docker container on AWS ECS:

bashCopy code

```
ecs-cli compose up --cluster <cluster_name>
```

This command deploys a Docker containerized application to an ECS cluster on AWS, allowing for scalable and resilient execution of containerized workloads.

In summary, the historical evolution of big data architectures has been characterized by a transition from traditional relational databases to distributed computing frameworks and cloud-native architectures. The convergence of batch and stream processing, along with the adoption of containerization and cloud computing, has paved the way for the development of highly scalable, agile, and cost-effective big data solutions that can meet the evolving needs of modern organizations. By staying abreast of current trends and advancements in big data technologies, organizations can leverage these architectures to unlock the full potential of their data assets and drive business growth and innovation.

Chapter 2: Understanding Scalability in Big Data Systems

The scalability of big data systems is crucial for handling the ever-increasing volume, velocity, and variety of data generated by modern applications and devices. As organizations strive to extract valuable insights from massive datasets, they encounter several scalability challenges that must be addressed to ensure the efficient processing and analysis of data. Next, we will explore the scalability challenges faced by big data systems and discuss strategies for overcoming these challenges to build robust and scalable data processing pipelines.

Volume Scalability: One of the primary challenges in big data systems is volume scalability, which refers to the ability to efficiently process and analyze large volumes of data. As the volume of data grows exponentially, traditional data processing systems struggle to scale effectively, leading to performance bottlenecks and increased processing times. To address this challenge, organizations need to adopt distributed computing frameworks like Apache Hadoop and Apache Spark, which enable parallel processing of data across clusters of commodity hardware. These frameworks leverage techniques like data partitioning and sharding to distribute data processing tasks across multiple nodes, allowing for horizontal scalability and improved performance.

CLI command to scale up the number of worker nodes in an Apache Spark cluster:

bashCopy code

```
spark-submit --master <master_url> --num-executors
<num_executors>                    --executor-cores
<cores_per_executor>              --executor-memory
<memory_per_executor> <path_to_jar> <arguments>
```

This command scales up the number of worker nodes in an Apache Spark cluster by specifying the desired number of executors, cores per executor, and memory per executor.

Velocity Scalability: Velocity scalability refers to the ability to process and analyze data streams in real-time or near-real-time. With the advent of IoT devices, social media platforms, and online transactions, organizations are inundated with vast streams of data that need to be processed and analyzed in a timely manner to extract actionable insights. Traditional batch processing systems are ill-suited for handling real-time data streams, as they introduce latency and processing delays. To achieve velocity scalability, organizations need to adopt stream processing frameworks like Apache Kafka and Apache Flink, which enable the ingestion, processing, and analysis of data streams in real-time.

CLI command to create a Kafka topic:

bashCopy code

```
kafka-topics.sh  --create  --topic  <topic_name>  --
bootstrap-server     <broker_list>      --partitions
```

<num_partitions>   --replication-factor
<replication_factor>
This command creates a Kafka topic with the specified name, number of partitions, and replication factor, allowing for the ingestion of data streams.

Variety Scalability: Variety scalability refers to the ability to handle diverse types of data, including structured, semi-structured, and unstructured data. In today's data-driven world, organizations collect data from a wide range of sources, including databases, log files, sensor data, social media feeds, and more. Traditional relational databases are limited in their ability to handle diverse data types and schemas, making it challenging to integrate and analyze heterogeneous data sources. To achieve variety scalability, organizations need to adopt flexible data storage and processing solutions like NoSQL databases and data lakes, which can accommodate a wide variety of data formats and schemas.

CLI command to create a table in Cassandra:
bashCopy code

```
cqlsh        -e        "CREATE        TABLE
<keyspace_name>.<table_name>        (<column1>
<data_type>, <column2> <data_type>, ...);"
```

This command creates a table in Cassandra with the specified keyspace, table name, columns, and data types, allowing for the storage of diverse data types.

Resource Management: Another scalability challenge in big data systems is resource management, which involves efficiently allocating and managing compute, storage, and network resources to meet the demands of data processing workloads. In distributed computing environments, resource contention and imbalance can lead to performance degradation and bottlenecks, impacting the overall scalability and reliability of the system. To address resource management challenges, organizations need to implement dynamic resource allocation and scheduling mechanisms, such as Apache YARN and Kubernetes, which can dynamically adjust resource allocations based on workload requirements and cluster utilization.

CLI command to scale up Kubernetes pods:

bashCopy code

```
kubectl scale --replicas=<num_replicas> deployment/<deployment_name>
```

This command scales up the number of replicas for a Kubernetes deployment, allowing for dynamic resource allocation and scaling based on workload demands.

In summary, scalability is a critical aspect of big data systems, enabling organizations to efficiently process and analyze massive volumes of data across diverse data sources. By addressing scalability challenges through the adoption of distributed computing frameworks, stream processing systems, flexible data storage solutions, and dynamic resource management techniques, organizations can build robust and scalable data processing pipelines that can meet the evolving demands of modern data-driven applications.

In the realm of scalable computing systems, two primary techniques are employed to address the ever-increasing demands of processing power, storage, and throughput: horizontal scalability and vertical scalability. These techniques serve as fundamental pillars in the design and deployment of scalable architectures, allowing organizations to efficiently scale their infrastructure to meet growing workloads and user demands. Next, we will delve into the concepts of horizontal and vertical scalability, explore their respective advantages and limitations, and discuss the deployment strategies and CLI commands associated with each technique.

Horizontal Scalability:

Horizontal scalability, also known as scale-out architecture, involves adding more hardware resources to a system by distributing the workload across multiple machines or nodes. Instead of upgrading individual components to handle increased demand, horizontal scalability achieves scalability by adding more instances of the same components in parallel. This approach offers several benefits, including improved fault tolerance, better resource utilization, and linear scalability, where performance scales linearly with the addition of more nodes.

One of the most common implementations of horizontal scalability is the deployment of distributed computing frameworks such as Apache Hadoop and

Apache Spark. These frameworks allow organizations to distribute data processing tasks across a cluster of commodity hardware, enabling parallel execution of computations and efficient utilization of resources. To deploy a horizontally scalable architecture using Apache Spark, organizations can leverage CLI commands to provision and manage Spark clusters across multiple nodes.

CLI command to deploy an Apache Spark cluster using the spark-submit command:

bashCopy code

```
spark-submit --deploy-mode cluster --master yarn --num-executors <num_executors> --executor-memory <memory_per_executor> --executor-cores <cores_per_executor> <path_to_application_jar> <application_arguments>
```

This command submits a Spark application to a YARN-managed cluster, specifying the number of executors, memory per executor, and cores per executor to allocate for the application.

Vertical Scalability:

Vertical scalability, also known as scale-up architecture, involves increasing the capacity of individual hardware components, such as CPU, memory, or storage, to handle increased workloads. Instead of adding more machines to the system, vertical scalability focuses on upgrading existing hardware resources to meet growing demands. While vertical scalability offers simplicity and ease of management, it has limitations in terms of scalability and cost-effectiveness, as there is a practical limit to the capacity of individual hardware components.

Organizations can implement vertical scalability techniques by upgrading hardware resources, such as adding more RAM or upgrading to a higher-capacity CPU. Additionally, virtualization technologies like VMware and Hyper-V allow organizations to dynamically allocate and scale resources across virtual machines, enabling flexible resource management and optimization. CLI commands are often used to manage virtual machines and allocate resources in virtualized environments.

CLI command to resize a virtual machine in VMware:
bashCopy code

```
vmware-cmd    <path_to_virtual_machine>    resize
<new_disk_size>
```

This command resizes a virtual machine disk to the specified size, allowing organizations to increase the capacity of virtual machines to accommodate growing workloads.

Deployment Strategies: When choosing between horizontal and vertical scalability, organizations should consider factors such as workload characteristics, performance requirements, and cost considerations. In general, horizontal scalability is favored for distributed data processing workloads that require high throughput and fault tolerance, while vertical scalability is suitable for applications with predictable workloads and resource requirements.

Organizations can also employ a combination of horizontal and vertical scalability techniques, known as hybrid scalability, to achieve the optimal balance between performance, scalability, and cost-efficiency. By leveraging the strengths of both horizontal and vertical scalability, organizations can build resilient and flexible architectures that can adapt to changing business needs and scale gracefully with growing workloads. In summary, horizontal and vertical scalability techniques play a crucial role in the design and deployment of scalable computing systems. While horizontal scalability offers the advantages of fault tolerance, resource utilization, and linear scalability, vertical scalability provides simplicity and ease of management. By understanding the principles and deployment strategies associated with each technique, organizations can build robust and scalable architectures that can meet the demands of modern data-intensive applications.

Chapter 3: Data Storage Architectures

In the landscape of modern computing, data storage technologies play a pivotal role in managing and storing vast amounts of data generated by various applications and systems. From traditional relational databases to distributed file systems and cloud storage solutions, a plethora of storage technologies exist to address different data storage requirements and use cases. Next, we will explore the diverse array of data storage technologies, their characteristics, deployment strategies, and CLI commands associated with their deployment and management.

Relational Databases:

Relational databases have long been a cornerstone of data storage and management, providing a structured and organized approach to storing data in tables with predefined schemas. Technologies such as MySQL, PostgreSQL, and Oracle Database are widely used for managing structured data in transactional and analytical workloads. To deploy a relational database, organizations can utilize CLI commands to provision database instances, create tables, and perform data manipulation tasks.

CLI command to create a table in MySQL:

bashCopy code

```
mysql -u <username> -p <password> -e "CREATE
TABLE     <table_name>     (<column1_name>
```

<column1_datatype>, <column2_name> <column2_datatype>, ...);"

This command connects to a MySQL database instance and executes a SQL statement to create a new table with specified columns and data types.

NoSQL Databases:

NoSQL databases have gained prominence in recent years for their ability to handle large volumes of unstructured and semi-structured data with flexibility and scalability. Technologies such as MongoDB, Cassandra, and Redis offer various data models, including document-oriented, column-family, and key-value stores, to cater to diverse application requirements. CLI commands are often used to manage NoSQL databases, such as creating collections, inserting documents, and querying data.

CLI command to insert a document in MongoDB:

bashCopy code

```
mongo            <database_name>            --eval
"db.<collection_name>.insert({<field1>:    <value1>,
<field2>: <value2>, ...});"
```

This command connects to a MongoDB database instance and inserts a new document into the specified collection.

Distributed File Systems:

Distributed file systems provide scalable and fault-tolerant storage solutions for large-scale data processing and analytics workloads. Technologies like Hadoop Distributed File System (HDFS) and Amazon S3 enable organizations to store and process petabytes of data across clusters of commodity hardware or cloud infrastructure. CLI commands are essential for managing distributed file systems, including uploading files, setting permissions, and monitoring storage usage.

CLI command to upload a file to Amazon S3:

bashCopy code

```
aws s3 cp <local_file_path> s3://<bucket_name>/<remote_file_path>
```

This command uses the AWS CLI to upload a file from the local file system to an Amazon S3 bucket.

Cloud Storage:

Cloud storage solutions offer scalable and cost-effective options for storing and managing data in the cloud. Providers like Amazon Web Services (AWS), Microsoft Azure, and Google Cloud Platform (GCP) offer a range of storage services, including object storage, block storage, and archival storage, with features such as high availability, durability, and security. CLI commands are widely used to interact with cloud storage services, such as creating buckets, uploading files, and managing storage policies.

CLI command to create a bucket in AWS S3:

bashCopy code

```
aws s3 mb s3://<bucket_name>
```

This command creates a new bucket in Amazon S3 using the AWS CLI.

In summary, data storage technologies encompass a diverse range of solutions tailored to meet the evolving needs of modern applications and systems.

Whether it's relational databases for structured data, NoSQL databases for unstructured data, distributed file systems for big data processing, or cloud storage for scalable and cost-effective storage, organizations have a multitude of options to choose from. By understanding the characteristics, deployment strategies, and CLI commands associated with each storage technology, organizations can architect robust and scalable storage solutions to meet their data storage and management requirements.

In the realm of distributed computing and big data processing, the efficient and scalable management of vast amounts of data is paramount. Distributed file systems and object stores are two prominent technologies that have emerged to address the challenges associated with storing and processing large datasets across distributed environments. Next, we will delve into the concepts, characteristics, deployment strategies, and CLI commands associated with distributed file systems and object stores.

Distributed File Systems:

Distributed file systems (DFS) are designed to store and manage large files across multiple nodes in a distributed environment. These systems provide high availability, fault tolerance, and scalability by distributing data across multiple storage nodes and replicating data to ensure data reliability. One of the most well-known distributed file systems is the Hadoop Distributed File System (HDFS), which is widely used in big data processing frameworks such as Apache Hadoop and Apache Spark.

To deploy HDFS, organizations typically set up a cluster of commodity hardware nodes, each running HDFS daemons responsible for storing and managing data blocks. CLI commands are used to interact with HDFS, including commands for file manipulation, cluster management, and monitoring.

CLI command to upload a file to HDFS:

bashCopy code

```
hdfs dfs -put <local_file_path> <hdfs_directory_path>
```

This command uploads a file from the local file system to the specified directory in HDFS.

Object Stores:

Object stores, also known as object-based storage systems, provide a scalable and efficient way to store and retrieve unstructured data objects, such as images, videos, documents, and log files. Unlike traditional file systems that organize data in a hierarchical structure, object stores organize data as objects with unique identifiers (keys) and metadata. Object stores offer advantages such as infinite scalability, low latency access, and built-in redundancy for data durability.

Amazon Simple Storage Service (S3) is one of the most popular object storage services, offering features such as versioning, lifecycle management, and fine-grained access control. To deploy an object store like Amazon S3, organizations can use cloud service providers' management consoles or CLI commands.

CLI command to create a bucket in Amazon S3:
bashCopy code
aws s3 mb s3://<bucket_name>
This command creates a new bucket in Amazon S3 using the AWS CLI.

Comparison:
While both distributed file systems and object stores are designed to handle large-scale data storage and processing, they differ in their architecture, data model, and use cases. Distributed file systems are optimized for storing and processing large files, making them well-suited for batch processing and analytics workloads. In contrast, object stores are ideal for storing and retrieving unstructured data objects and are commonly used in web applications, content delivery networks (CDNs), and data lakes.

Distributed file systems and object stores are foundational components of modern data storage and processing architectures, providing organizations with the scalability, reliability, and flexibility needed to manage big data effectively. By understanding the concepts, deployment strategies, and CLI commands associated with distributed file systems and object stores, organizations can architect robust and scalable storage solutions to meet their data storage and processing requirements.

Chapter 4: Distributed Computing and Processing

In the landscape of big data processing, the MapReduce paradigm has emerged as a fundamental framework for parallel and distributed computing. Developed by Google in the early 2000s, MapReduce revolutionized the way large-scale data processing tasks are executed across clusters of commodity hardware. Next, we will explore the MapReduce paradigm, its core principles, variants, and the CLI commands used to deploy MapReduce applications.

Introduction to MapReduce:

At its core, MapReduce is a programming model for processing and generating large datasets in parallel across distributed clusters. The paradigm consists of two main phases: the Map phase and the Reduce phase. In the Map phase, input data is divided into smaller chunks, processed independently in parallel by multiple worker nodes, and transformed into intermediate key-value pairs. In the Reduce phase, the intermediate key-value pairs are shuffled and sorted, and then aggregated based on keys to produce the final output.

MapReduce applications are typically deployed on distributed computing frameworks such as Apache Hadoop, which provides a distributed file system (HDFS) for data storage and a resource manager (YARN) for job scheduling and cluster resource management.

CLI command to run a MapReduce job on Hadoop:
bashCopy code
hadoop jar <path_to_jar_file> <main_class_name> <input_directory> <output_directory>
This command runs a MapReduce job on a Hadoop cluster, specifying the input and output directories for data processing.

Variants of MapReduce:

While the classic MapReduce paradigm laid the foundation for distributed data processing, several variants and extensions have been developed to address specific use cases and optimize performance. One notable variant is Apache Spark, which introduces in-memory processing and a more flexible programming model compared to traditional MapReduce.

Apache Spark leverages resilient distributed datasets (RDDs) and a directed acyclic graph (DAG) execution engine to achieve faster processing speeds and better fault tolerance. Spark provides high-level APIs in multiple languages, including Scala, Java, Python, and R, making it accessible to a wider audience of developers and data scientists.

CLI command to submit a Spark job:
bashCopy code
spark-submit --class <main_class_name> --master <master_url> <path_to_jar_file> <input_directory> <output_directory>

This command submits a Spark job to a cluster, specifying the main class, master URL, input, and output directories.

Another variant of MapReduce is Apache Flink, which offers low-latency stream processing capabilities in addition to batch processing. Flink's stream processing model enables real-time analytics and event-driven applications, making it suitable for use cases such as fraud detection, real-time monitoring, and IoT data processing.

CLI command to execute a Flink job:

bashCopy code

```
flink run <path_to_jar_file> --input <input_file> --output <output_directory>
```

This command executes a Flink job, specifying the input file and output directory for data processing.

The MapReduce paradigm and its variants have revolutionized the field of big data processing, enabling organizations to efficiently analyze and derive insights from large datasets. By understanding the core principles of MapReduce and exploring its variants such as Apache Spark and Apache Flink, organizations can leverage these technologies to build scalable, fault-tolerant, and high-performance data processing pipelines for a wide range of use cases.

The Spark Framework, renowned for its in-memory computing capabilities, has emerged as a cornerstone technology in the realm of big data processing. This chapter delves into the intricacies of the Spark

Framework, its underlying architecture, key features, deployment techniques, and CLI commands essential for leveraging its immense potential in processing large-scale datasets.

Introduction to the Spark Framework:

Apache Spark, an open-source distributed computing framework, provides a unified platform for processing and analyzing large volumes of data in a distributed manner. Unlike traditional MapReduce frameworks, Spark employs an in-memory computing model, enabling significantly faster processing speeds by caching intermediate data in memory.

Spark's Core Components:

At the heart of the Spark Framework lie several core components that facilitate distributed data processing:

Resilient Distributed Datasets (RDDs): RDDs serve as the fundamental abstraction in Spark, representing distributed collections of data that can be operated on in parallel. RDDs are immutable and fault-tolerant, enabling fault recovery through lineage-based recomputation.

Spark SQL: Spark SQL offers a high-level API for interacting with structured data using SQL queries and DataFrame abstractions. It seamlessly integrates with Spark's core engine, allowing users to perform complex data transformations and analytics tasks with ease.

Spark Streaming: Spark Streaming extends Spark's capabilities to process real-time data streams. It ingests data from various sources, such as Kafka or Flume, and processes it in micro-batch intervals, enabling real-time analytics and processing of streaming data.

MLlib (Machine Learning Library): MLlib is a scalable machine learning library built on top of Spark, providing a rich set of algorithms and utilities for performing machine learning tasks such as classification, regression, clustering, and collaborative filtering.

GraphX: GraphX is a graph processing library integrated into Spark, designed for analyzing and processing large-scale graph data. It provides an expressive API for building graph algorithms and performing graph analytics tasks.

Deployment of Spark Applications:

Deploying Spark applications involves setting up a Spark cluster and submitting jobs to the cluster for execution. Spark supports various deployment modes, including standalone mode, YARN mode, and Mesos mode.

Standalone mode is the simplest deployment option, where Spark applications run on a dedicated cluster managed by the Spark cluster manager. YARN mode leverages Apache Hadoop YARN for resource management and job scheduling, enabling seamless integration with existing Hadoop clusters.

CLI Commands for Spark Application Deployment:

Running a Spark Application in Standalone Mode:

bashCopy code

```
spark-submit                          --master
spark://<master_ip>:<master_port>        --class
<main_class>    <application_jar>    <input_path>
<output_path>
```

This command submits a Spark application to a standalone Spark cluster, specifying the master node's IP address and port, main class, application JAR file, input path, and output path.

Running a Spark Application in YARN Mode:

bashCopy code

```
spark-submit --master yarn --deploy-mode cluster --class <main_class> <application_jar> <input_path> <output_path>
```

This command submits a Spark application to a YARN cluster, specifying the master as yarn, deploy mode as cluster, main class, application JAR file, input path, and output path.

The Spark Framework's in-memory computing capabilities have revolutionized big data processing, enabling organizations to achieve unprecedented levels of performance and scalability in their data analytics workflows. By understanding the core components, deployment options, and CLI commands associated with Spark, data engineers and scientists can harness its power to build robust, high-performance data processing pipelines for a wide range of use cases.

Chapter 5: High Availability and Fault Tolerance

High availability (HA) is a critical aspect of big data systems, ensuring uninterrupted access to data and services even in the face of failures or outages. This chapter explores the principles of high availability in big data systems, covering key concepts, strategies, and techniques to achieve robust and fault-tolerant architectures.

Introduction to High Availability:

High availability refers to the ability of a system to remain operational and accessible for extended periods, typically measured as a percentage of uptime over a given time frame. In the context of big data systems, high availability is essential to ensure continuous data processing, analytics, and access to services, thereby minimizing downtime and ensuring business continuity.

Principles of High Availability:

Redundancy: Redundancy is a fundamental principle in achieving high availability, involving the duplication of critical components, resources, or services to mitigate the impact of failures. Redundant components, such as servers, storage devices, and network links, are deployed in a distributed manner to ensure fault tolerance and resilience.

Fault Tolerance: Fault tolerance mechanisms are designed to detect and recover from failures automatically, ensuring the uninterrupted operation of the system. Techniques such as replication, data mirroring, and automatic failover mechanisms are employed to maintain service continuity in the event of hardware or software failures.

Load Balancing: Load balancing distributes incoming traffic or workload across multiple servers or resources to optimize resource utilization, improve performance, and prevent overload or bottlenecks. Dynamic load balancing algorithms monitor system metrics and traffic patterns, dynamically adjusting the distribution of requests to ensure optimal performance and availability.

Disaster Recovery: Disaster recovery strategies are essential for mitigating the impact of catastrophic events such as natural disasters, cyber attacks, or hardware failures. Disaster recovery plans include backup and restore procedures, off-site replication of data, and failover mechanisms to secondary data centers or cloud environments.

Scalability: Scalability is a key consideration in designing highly available systems, enabling them to accommodate growing workloads and user demands without sacrificing performance or reliability. Scalability can be achieved through horizontal scaling (adding more nodes or resources) or vertical scaling (upgrading existing resources).

Deployment of Highly Available Systems:

Deploying highly available systems involves implementing redundant components, fault tolerance mechanisms, and robust disaster recovery strategies. The choice of deployment architecture depends on factors such as budget, performance requirements, data center locations, and regulatory compliance.

CLI Commands for High Availability Deployment:

Configuration of Load Balancers:

bashCopy code

```
sudo apt-get install nginx
```

This command installs the Nginx web server, which can be configured as a load balancer to distribute incoming traffic across multiple backend servers for improved availability and scalability.

Setup of Replication in Database Systems:

bashCopy code

```
CREATE DATABASE my_database;
```

This SQL command creates a new database named my_database. To achieve high availability and fault tolerance, database replication can be configured to replicate data across multiple database instances, ensuring data consistency and redundancy.

High availability is paramount in ensuring the reliability, resilience, and continuous operation of big data systems. By adhering to principles such as redundancy, fault tolerance, load balancing, disaster recovery, and scalability, organizations can build robust architectures capable of withstanding failures and maintaining uninterrupted service delivery. The deployment of highly available systems requires careful planning, configuration, and monitoring to mitigate risks and ensure seamless operation in the face of challenges.

Fault tolerance mechanisms and failover strategies are essential components of modern computing systems, particularly in the context of big data where the uninterrupted processing and availability of data are paramount. This chapter delves into the principles, techniques, and best practices for achieving fault tolerance and implementing effective failover strategies in big data environments.

Introduction to Fault Tolerance:

Fault tolerance is the ability of a system to continue operating and providing services in the presence of faults, errors, or failures. In big data systems, which often involve distributed architectures and massive datasets, ensuring fault tolerance is critical to maintaining data integrity, reliability, and availability.

Principles of Fault Tolerance:

Redundancy: Redundancy is a cornerstone principle of fault tolerance, involving the duplication of critical components, resources, or services within a system. By deploying redundant components such as servers, storage devices, and network links, organizations can mitigate the impact of failures and ensure continuous operation.

Replication: Replication involves creating and maintaining copies of data across multiple nodes or systems, thereby enhancing fault tolerance and data availability. In distributed databases and storage systems, data replication ensures that data remains accessible even if individual nodes or components fail.

Error Detection and Correction: Fault tolerance mechanisms incorporate error detection and correction techniques to identify and rectify errors before they escalate into failures. Error detection mechanisms such as checksums, parity checks, and redundancy checks help detect data corruption or transmission errors, while error correction algorithms such as RAID (Redundant Array of Independent Disks) can restore data integrity.

Automatic Failover: Automatic failover is a proactive strategy for minimizing downtime and service disruptions by automatically redirecting traffic or workload to redundant or standby components in the event of a failure. Failover mechanisms detect failures in real-time and seamlessly transition to backup systems or resources to maintain service continuity.

Load Balancing: Load balancing distributes incoming traffic or workload across multiple servers or resources to optimize resource utilization, prevent overloads, and improve fault tolerance. Load balancers monitor the health and performance of backend servers, dynamically adjusting traffic distribution to ensure optimal performance and availability.

Deployment of Fault Tolerance Mechanisms:

Deploying fault tolerance mechanisms involves configuring redundant components, implementing replication strategies, and setting up failover mechanisms to ensure continuous operation and data availability. Organizations must carefully design and test their fault tolerance strategies to identify and mitigate potential points of failure.

CLI Commands for Fault Tolerance Deployment:

Configuration of RAID:

bashCopy code

```
sudo mdadm --create /dev/md0 --level=1 --raid-devices=2 /dev/sda /dev/sdb
```

This command creates a RAID 1 (mirroring) array named /dev/md0 using two devices (/dev/sda and /dev/sdb), providing redundancy and fault tolerance by maintaining identical copies of data on both disks.

Setup of Automatic Failover in Network Load Balancers:

bashCopy code

```
aws elb create-lb \ --name my-load-balancer \ --subnets subnet-12345678 subnet-87654321 \ --listeners "Protocol=HTTP,LoadBalancerPort=80,InstanceProtocol=HTTP,InstancePort=80" \ --scheme internet-facing
```

This AWS CLI command creates a network load balancer named my-load-balancer with automatic failover enabled, distributing incoming HTTP traffic across multiple backend instances for improved fault tolerance and availability.

Fault tolerance mechanisms and failover strategies are indispensable components of modern big data systems, ensuring continuous operation, data integrity, and availability in the face of failures or disruptions. By embracing principles such as redundancy, replication, error detection, automatic failover, and load balancing, organizations can build resilient architectures capable of withstanding faults and maintaining service continuity. The deployment of fault tolerance mechanisms requires careful planning, configuration, and testing to mitigate risks and ensure optimal performance and reliability.

Chapter 6: Data Governance and Security

Data governance plays a pivotal role in the successful management, utilization, and protection of data assets within big data environments. This chapter explores the importance of data governance, its key principles, and strategies for implementation to ensure data integrity, compliance, and trustworthiness.

Understanding Data Governance:

Data governance refers to the framework, policies, processes, and controls implemented to manage and safeguard data assets across an organization. It encompasses various aspects such as data quality, security, privacy, compliance, and access control, aiming to ensure that data is accurate, consistent, secure, and compliant with regulatory requirements.

The Importance of Data Governance in Big Data Environments:

Data Quality Assurance: Data governance ensures the accuracy, completeness, and reliability of data by establishing standards, procedures, and validation mechanisms for data acquisition, storage, and processing. By enforcing data quality controls and governance policies, organizations can enhance the trustworthiness and usability of big data assets for decision-making and analytics.

Regulatory Compliance: In today's regulatory landscape, organizations are subject to stringent data protection and privacy regulations such as GDPR, CCPA, HIPAA, and PCI DSS. Data governance frameworks help organizations achieve and maintain regulatory compliance by implementing policies, controls, and audit trails to track data usage, access, and consent.

Risk Management: Effective data governance mitigates risks associated with data breaches, unauthorized access, data loss, and non-compliance. By defining data ownership, access controls, and encryption policies, organizations can reduce the likelihood of security incidents and protect sensitive data from unauthorized disclosure or misuse.

Decision-Making and Analytics: High-quality, reliable data is essential for accurate decision-making and insightful analytics. Data governance ensures that data is consistent, trustworthy, and relevant, enabling organizations to derive meaningful insights, identify trends, and make informed business decisions based on reliable data.

Data Collaboration and Sharing: Data governance frameworks facilitate collaboration and data sharing among internal stakeholders, departments, and external partners while ensuring data security and privacy. By defining data ownership, rights, and responsibilities, organizations can foster a culture of data stewardship and collaboration, driving innovation and efficiency.

Implementation Strategies for Data Governance:

Define Data Governance Policies and Standards: Establish clear policies, standards, and guidelines for data management, including data classification, metadata management, data retention, and access controls. Define roles and responsibilities for data stewards, data owners, and data custodians to ensure accountability and compliance.

Implement Data Governance Tools and Technologies: Deploy data governance tools and technologies to automate and enforce data governance policies, controls, and workflows. Utilize data cataloging, metadata management, data lineage, and data quality tools to discover, document, and govern data assets across the organization.

Educate and Train Data Users: Educate employees, stakeholders, and data users on data governance principles, policies, and best practices through training programs, workshops, and awareness campaigns. Foster a data-driven culture and promote awareness of the importance of data governance in achieving organizational goals.

Establish Data Governance Committees: Form cross-functional data governance committees or councils to oversee the implementation and enforcement of data governance initiatives. Include representatives from IT, legal, compliance, risk management, and business units to ensure alignment with organizational objectives and priorities.

CLI Commands for Data Governance Implementation:

Implementation of Access Controls:

```bash
Copy code
chmod 755 file.txt
```

This command sets the file permissions of file.txt to read, write, and execute for the owner, and read and execute for group members and others, ensuring controlled access to sensitive data files.

Deployment of Encryption Policies:

```bash
Copy code
gpg --encrypt --recipient user@example.com file.txt
```

This command encrypts file.txt using GNU Privacy Guard (GPG), ensuring the confidentiality and integrity of the data during transmission or storage.

Data governance is essential for managing, protecting, and deriving value from data assets within big data environments. By implementing robust data governance frameworks, organizations can ensure data integrity, compliance, security, and trustworthiness, driving informed decision-making, regulatory compliance, risk management, and collaboration. The deployment of data governance requires a holistic approach, encompassing policies, processes, technologies, and organizational culture to effectively govern data throughout its lifecycle and derive maximum value from data assets.

Security challenges in big data architectures present significant concerns for organizations aiming to safeguard sensitive data from unauthorized access, breaches, and malicious activities. This chapter delves into the myriad security challenges faced by big data architectures and explores various solutions and best practices to mitigate these risks effectively.

Understanding Security Challenges in Big Data Architectures:

Data Breaches and Unauthorized Access: Big data architectures often store vast amounts of sensitive information, making them lucrative targets for cybercriminals. Unauthorized access to data can lead to data breaches, resulting in financial losses, reputational damage, and legal repercussions for organizations.

Data Privacy and Compliance: Regulatory requirements such as GDPR, CCPA, HIPAA, and PCI DSS mandate stringent data privacy measures to protect personally identifiable information (PII) and ensure consumer privacy rights. Non-compliance with these regulations can result in hefty fines and penalties for organizations.

Insider Threats: Insider threats pose a significant risk to data security, as malicious insiders or negligent employees may intentionally or inadvertently compromise sensitive data. Organizations must implement robust access controls, monitoring mechanisms, and employee training programs to mitigate insider threats effectively.

Distributed Data Storage and Processing: Distributed data storage and processing in big data architectures introduce complexities and vulnerabilities, as data is fragmented across multiple nodes and processed in distributed environments. Ensuring data integrity, confidentiality, and availability becomes challenging in such decentralized infrastructures.

Scalability and Performance Trade-offs: Security measures implemented to protect big data environments may introduce performance overhead and scalability limitations, impacting system performance and user experience. Balancing security requirements with scalability and performance considerations is essential to maintain operational efficiency.

Solutions and Best Practices for Security in Big Data Architectures:

Encryption: Implement encryption techniques such as data-at-rest encryption, data-in-transit encryption, and end-to-end encryption to protect data from unauthorized access and interception. Use encryption algorithms such as AES and RSA to encrypt sensitive data stored in databases, file systems, and communication channels.

Access Control and Authentication: Enforce strict access controls and authentication mechanisms to restrict access to sensitive data and resources based on user roles, privileges, and authentication factors. Deploy technologies such as LDAP, Kerberos, OAuth, and multi-factor authentication (MFA) to authenticate users and authorize access to data.

Data Masking and Anonymization: Apply data masking and anonymization techniques to obfuscate sensitive information in non-production environments, minimizing the risk of unauthorized exposure during development, testing, and training activities. Use tools and algorithms such as tokenization, pseudonymization, and differential privacy to anonymize PII and sensitive data.

Auditing and Logging: Implement comprehensive auditing and logging mechanisms to track and monitor user activities, data access, and system events within big data environments. Utilize centralized logging solutions and security information and event management (SIEM) platforms to collect, analyze, and correlate security logs for anomaly detection and incident response.

Threat Detection and Response: Deploy advanced threat detection and response solutions such as intrusion detection systems (IDS), intrusion prevention systems (IPS), and security analytics platforms to identify and mitigate security threats in real-time. Utilize machine learning and AI-driven techniques to detect anomalous behavior, suspicious activities, and potential security incidents proactively.

CLI Commands for Security Implementation in Big Data Architectures:

Encryption of Data-at-Rest:

bashCopy code

```
openssl enc -aes-256-cbc -salt -in data.txt -out encrypted_data.enc
```

This command encrypts the data stored in data.txt using the AES-256-CBC encryption algorithm and saves the encrypted data to encrypted_data.enc, ensuring data confidentiality when stored at rest.

Access Control Configuration:

bashCopy code

chmod 600 file.txt

This command sets the file permissions of file.txt to read and write for the owner only, restricting access to the file to authorized users and enhancing data security.

Security challenges in big data architectures necessitate robust measures and best practices to safeguard sensitive data from threats, breaches, and vulnerabilities. By implementing encryption, access controls, authentication mechanisms, data masking, auditing, threat detection, and response solutions, organizations can mitigate security risks effectively and ensure the confidentiality, integrity, and availability of data within big data environments. CLI commands and security best practices play a crucial role in securing big data architectures and protecting against evolving cyber threats and compliance requirements.

Chapter 7: Cloud Computing for Big Data

Cloud computing has revolutionized the way organizations process, store, and analyze big data by providing scalable and cost-effective solutions through various service models. This chapter explores the different cloud service models for big data processing, including Infrastructure as a Service (IaaS), Platform as a Service (PaaS), and Software as a Service (SaaS), along with their deployment considerations, benefits, and use cases.

Understanding Cloud Service Models for Big Data Processing:

Infrastructure as a Service (IaaS): IaaS offers virtualized computing resources over the internet, allowing organizations to provision and manage infrastructure components such as virtual machines, storage, and networking on-demand. Cloud providers, such as Amazon Web Services (AWS), Microsoft Azure, and Google Cloud Platform (GCP), deliver scalable infrastructure resources to support big data processing workloads. Users have full control over the underlying infrastructure and can deploy operating systems, databases, and big data frameworks according to their requirements.

Platform as a Service (PaaS): PaaS abstracts the underlying infrastructure and provides a platform for developers to build, deploy, and manage applications without worrying about hardware and software provisioning. PaaS offerings include managed services for big data processing, such as Hadoop as a Service, Spark as a Service, and NoSQL databases, enabling developers to focus on application development and data analysis tasks. Cloud providers manage the underlying infrastructure, including hardware, networking, and middleware, while users leverage high-level APIs and development tools to streamline the development process.

Software as a Service (SaaS): SaaS delivers software applications over the internet on a subscription basis, eliminating the need for organizations to install, maintain, and upgrade software locally. SaaS solutions for big data processing include analytics platforms, data visualization tools, and business intelligence applications that enable users to derive insights from large datasets without managing infrastructure or writing code. SaaS offerings simplify access to advanced analytics capabilities and empower business users to make data-driven decisions using intuitive interfaces and dashboards.

Benefits of Cloud Service Models for Big Data Processing:

Scalability: Cloud service models offer scalability and elasticity to accommodate fluctuating workloads and growing data volumes. Users can scale resources up or down dynamically based on demand, ensuring optimal performance and cost-efficiency for big data processing tasks.

Cost-effectiveness: Cloud computing provides a pay-as-you-go pricing model, allowing organizations to pay only for the resources and services they consume. By leveraging cloud service models for big data processing, organizations can reduce capital expenses, minimize upfront investments in infrastructure, and achieve better cost predictability for their data analytics initiatives.

Flexibility and Agility: Cloud service models offer flexibility and agility to adapt to changing business requirements and technological advancements. Users can leverage a wide range of services and tools available on cloud platforms to experiment with different data processing techniques, integrate third-party services, and innovate rapidly without the constraints of traditional IT infrastructure.

Accessibility and Collaboration: Cloud-based big data processing solutions enable remote access and collaboration among distributed teams, allowing users to analyze data, share insights, and collaborate on projects in real-time from anywhere with an internet connection. Cloud platforms facilitate seamless data integration, collaboration, and knowledge sharing across departments and geographies, fostering a culture of data-driven decision-making within organizations.

Reliability and Resilience: Cloud providers operate redundant data centers with built-in redundancy, fault tolerance, and disaster recovery capabilities to ensure high availability and data resilience for big data processing workloads. By leveraging the reliability and resilience of cloud infrastructure, organizations can minimize downtime, mitigate data loss risks, and maintain business continuity in the event of hardware failures or natural disasters.

Use Cases and Deployment Considerations:

Real-time Analytics: Organizations can deploy real-time analytics solutions on cloud platforms to analyze streaming data from various sources, such as IoT devices, social media feeds, and transactional systems. Cloud-based stream processing frameworks like Apache Kafka and Apache Flink enable continuous data ingestion, processing, and analysis in real-time, empowering organizations to derive actionable insights and respond promptly to changing market conditions.

Batch Processing: Cloud service models support batch processing of large datasets using distributed computing frameworks like Apache Hadoop and Apache Spark. Organizations can leverage cloud-based Hadoop clusters and Spark clusters to parallelize data processing tasks, perform complex analytics operations, and generate insights from structured and unstructured data at scale. By utilizing managed big data services and serverless computing platforms, organizations can streamline batch processing workflows and optimize resource utilization for cost-effective data processing.

Data Warehousing and Business Intelligence: Cloud-based data warehousing solutions such as Amazon Redshift, Google BigQuery, and Snowflake provide scalable, high-performance platforms for storing and analyzing structured data. Organizations can migrate their on-premises data warehouses to the cloud or adopt cloud-native data warehouse solutions to unlock the full potential of their data assets. Cloud-based business intelligence tools and visualization platforms enable users to explore data, create interactive dashboards, and share insights across the organization, driving informed decision-making and strategic planning initiatives.

CLI Commands and Deployment Techniques:

Provisioning Virtual Machines (IaaS):

bashCopy code

```
az vm create --resource-group myResourceGroup --name myVM --image UbuntuLTS --admin-username azureuser --generate-ssh-keys
```

This command creates a virtual machine named myVM in the resource group myResourceGroup using the UbuntuLTS image, with the specified admin username and SSH key authentication.

Deploying Spark Cluster (PaaS):

bashCopy code

```
gcloud dataproc clusters create my-cluster --region us-central1 --num-workers 2 --machine-type n1-standard-4 --master-machine-type n1-standard-4 --initialization-actions gs://dataproc-initialization-actions/cloud-sql-proxy/cloud-sql-proxy.sh
```

This command creates a Dataproc cluster named my-cluster in the us-central1 region with two worker nodes, using n1-standard-4 machine types for both master and worker nodes, and initializes Cloud SQL proxy for accessing Google Cloud SQL databases.

Configuring Data Warehouse (SaaS):

bashCopy code

```
bq mk my_dataset
```

This command creates a BigQuery dataset named my_dataset in the default project, allowing users to store and query data in a structured format within the BigQuery data warehouse.

Cloud service models offer scalable, cost-effective, and flexible solutions for big data processing, enabling organizations to leverage advanced analytics capabilities, streamline workflows, and derive actionable insights from large and diverse datasets. By understanding the different cloud service models, benefits, use cases, and deployment considerations, organizations can harness the power of cloud computing to drive innovation, accelerate digital transformation, and gain a competitive edge in the data-driven economy.

With the increasing adoption of cloud computing for big data processing, organizations need effective deployment strategies to optimize performance, scalability, and cost-efficiency. This chapter explores various deployment strategies for deploying big data workloads in the cloud, including Infrastructure as Code (IaC), containerization, serverless computing, and hybrid cloud deployments.

Infrastructure as Code (IaC): Infrastructure as Code (IaC) is a DevOps practice that automates the provisioning and management of infrastructure resources using declarative or imperative code. By defining infrastructure configurations as code, organizations can automate the deployment of big data clusters, storage systems, and networking components in the cloud.

Tools like Terraform, AWS CloudFormation, and Azure Resource Manager enable users to define infrastructure configurations in reusable templates and deploy them consistently across different cloud environments. This approach ensures infrastructure consistency, repeatability, and scalability for big data workloads.

Containerization: Containerization is a lightweight virtualization technology that encapsulates applications and their dependencies into portable, self-contained units called containers. Docker is a popular containerization platform that enables organizations to package big data applications, libraries, and dependencies into Docker containers and deploy them across different cloud environments. Kubernetes, an open-source container orchestration platform, provides features for managing containerized workloads, scaling applications, and automating deployment workflows in cloud-native environments. By containerizing big data applications, organizations can achieve resource isolation, scalability, and flexibility while simplifying deployment and management tasks.

Serverless Computing: Serverless computing, also known as Function as a Service (FaaS), abstracts infrastructure management and enables organizations to execute code in stateless, ephemeral containers without provisioning or managing servers. Cloud providers like AWS Lambda, Azure Functions, and Google Cloud Functions offer serverless platforms for running event-driven, serverless workloads, including data processing tasks, real-time analytics, and batch processing jobs. Organizations can deploy big data workloads as serverless functions, trigger them in response to events or scheduled intervals, and pay only for the compute resources consumed during execution. Serverless computing offers benefits such as automatic scaling, reduced operational overhead, and cost-effective pricing models for sporadic or unpredictable workloads.

Hybrid Cloud Deployments: Hybrid cloud deployments involve the integration of on-premises infrastructure with public cloud resources to create a seamless and flexible computing environment. Organizations can deploy big data workloads in a hybrid cloud architecture by leveraging cloud bursting, data replication, and hybrid data processing frameworks. Cloud bursting allows organizations to extend their on-premises infrastructure to the cloud during peak demand periods, enabling them to scale resources dynamically and avoid performance bottlenecks. Data replication technologies such as AWS DataSync, Azure Data Factory, and Google Cloud Storage Transfer Service facilitate the seamless movement of data between on-premises data centers and cloud storage platforms, ensuring data consistency and availability across hybrid environments. Hybrid data processing frameworks like Apache Hadoop, Apache Spark, and Apache Flink support distributed processing of data across hybrid cloud infrastructures, enabling organizations to leverage the scalability and elasticity of the cloud while maintaining control over sensitive data and compliance requirements.

Deployment Techniques and CLI Commands:

Infrastructure as Code (IaC) Deployment:

bashCopy code

```
terraform init terraform plan terraform apply
```

These commands initialize Terraform, generate an execution plan, and apply the defined infrastructure configurations to create and provision cloud resources for big data workloads.

Containerization Deployment:

bashCopy code

```
docker build -t my-app . docker run -d --name my-container my-app
```

These commands build a Docker image for the big data application and run it in a Docker container, providing isolation, portability, and scalability for deploying big data workloads in containerized environments.

Serverless Computing Deployment:

bashCopy code

```
aws lambda create-function --function-name my-function --runtime python3.8 --handler lambda_function.lambda_handler --role arn:aws:iam::123456789012:role/service-role/my-role --code S3Bucket=my-bucket,S3Key=my-key.zip
```

This AWS CLI command creates a serverless function named my-function using AWS Lambda, specifying the runtime, handler, IAM role, and code location for deploying the big data workload as a serverless function.

Hybrid Cloud Deployment:

bashCopy code

```
azcopy copy "C:\local\data" "https://my-storage-account.blob.core.windows.net/my-container" --recursive=true
```

This Azure CLI command copies data from a local directory to a cloud storage container using AzCopy, facilitating data replication and synchronization between on-premises and cloud environments in a hybrid deployment scenario.

Effective deployment strategies are essential for deploying big data workloads in the cloud and leveraging the scalability, agility, and cost-efficiency of cloud computing platforms. By adopting Infrastructure as Code (IaC), containerization, serverless computing, and hybrid cloud deployments, organizations can streamline deployment processes, improve resource utilization, and accelerate time-to-market for their big data initiatives.CLI commands and deployment techniques play a crucial role in automating deployment workflows, ensuring infrastructure consistency, and optimizing performance for big data workloads in the cloud.

Chapter 8: Containerization and Orchestration

Containerization has revolutionized the way software applications are developed, deployed, and managed in modern IT environments. This chapter provides an in-depth exploration of containerization technologies, focusing on popular tools like Docker and Kubernetes. We'll delve into the fundamentals of containerization, the architecture of Docker and Kubernetes, and practical examples of deploying containerized applications.

Fundamentals of Containerization:

Containerization is a lightweight virtualization technology that encapsulates an application and its dependencies into a single, portable unit called a container. Unlike traditional virtual machines (VMs), containers share the host operating system kernel and run as isolated processes, providing consistency and efficiency across different environments. By packaging applications with their dependencies, containers ensure that software runs consistently regardless of the underlying infrastructure.

Docker:

Docker is a leading containerization platform that simplifies the process of building, distributing, and running containerized applications. It consists of three main components: Docker Engine, Docker Image, and Docker Container. Docker Engine is the runtime environment for containers, while Docker Image is a lightweight, standalone executable package that contains everything needed to run a piece of software. Docker Container is an instance of a Docker Image that runs in isolation and can be easily deployed and managed.

To deploy a containerized application with Docker, the following CLI commands can be used:

Build a Docker Image:

bashCopy code

```
docker build -t my-app .
```

This command builds a Docker image named "my-app" based on the Dockerfile located in the current directory.

Run a Docker Container:

bashCopy code

```
docker run -d --name my-container my-app
```

This command runs a Docker container named "my-container" based on the "my-app" image in detached mode.

View Docker Container Logs:

bashCopy code

```
docker logs my-container
```

This command displays the logs of the "my-container" Docker container.

Kubernetes:

Kubernetes, also known as K8s, is an open-source container orchestration platform for automating the deployment, scaling, and management of containerized applications. It provides features for container scheduling, service discovery, load balancing, and self-healing, making it ideal for deploying and managing complex microservices architectures.

Kubernetes architecture consists of several components, including the Kubernetes Master and Kubernetes Nodes. The Kubernetes Master is responsible for managing the cluster and coordinating communication between nodes, while Kubernetes Nodes are the worker machines responsible for running containers.

To deploy a containerized application with Kubernetes, the following CLI commands can be used:

Deploy a Kubernetes Pod:

bashCopy code

```
kubectl apply -f pod.yaml
```

This command deploys a Kubernetes Pod defined in the "pod.yaml" configuration file.

Scale Kubernetes Pods:

bashCopy code

```
kubectl scale --replicas=3 deployment/my-deployment
```

This command scales the number of replicas of a Kubernetes Deployment named "my-deployment" to three instances.

Expose Kubernetes Service:

bashCopy code

```
kubectl expose deployment my-deployment --type=LoadBalancer --port=80 --target-port=8080
```

This command exposes a Kubernetes Deployment named "my-deployment" as a LoadBalancer service on port 80, forwarding traffic to port 8080 on the pods.

Containerization technologies like Docker and Kubernetes have revolutionized the way software applications are developed, deployed, and managed. By providing lightweight, portable environments for running applications, containers offer numerous benefits, including increased agility, scalability, and resource utilization. With Docker simplifying the process of building and running containers and Kubernetes providing advanced orchestration capabilities for managing containerized workloads at scale, organizations can embrace containerization to accelerate their digital transformation journey.

Chapter 8: Containerization and Orchestration

Containerization has emerged as a transformative technology in the field of software development and deployment, enabling organizations to build, package, and deploy applications with unprecedented speed, efficiency, and scalability. This chapter provides an in-depth exploration of containerization technologies, focusing on two of the most prominent platforms: Docker and Kubernetes. We will delve into the fundamental concepts, architecture, and practical applications of these technologies, as well as provide insights into how they are revolutionizing modern IT infrastructures.

Fundamentals of Containerization:

At its core, containerization is a lightweight virtualization technology that allows developers to encapsulate an application and its dependencies into a single, portable unit called a container. Unlike traditional virtual machines (VMs), which require a separate operating system instance for each application, containers share the host operating system's kernel, resulting in greater efficiency and resource utilization. Containers provide a consistent runtime environment across different platforms, making it easier to develop, test, and deploy software applications.

Docker:

Docker is a leading containerization platform that has played a pivotal role in popularizing container technology. It provides developers with a comprehensive set of tools for building, distributing, and running containerized applications. The core components of Docker include Docker Engine, Docker Images, and Docker Containers. Docker Engine is the runtime environment for containers, while Docker Images are read-only templates that contain the application code, libraries, and dependencies. Docker Containers are lightweight, isolated instances of Docker Images that can be easily deployed and managed.

To deploy a containerized application with Docker, developers typically use the following CLI commands:

Build Docker Image:

bashCopy code

```
docker build -t myapp:v1 .
```

This command builds a Docker image named "myapp" with the tag "v1" based on the Dockerfile located in the current directory.

Run Docker Container:

bashCopy code

```
docker run -d -p 8080:80 myapp:v1
```

This command starts a Docker container based on the "myapp:v1" image in detached mode, mapping port 8080 on the host to port 80 on the container.

View Docker Container Logs:

bashCopy code

```
docker logs <container_id>
```

This command displays the logs of a running Docker container identified by its container ID.

Kubernetes:

Kubernetes is an open-source container orchestration platform that automates the deployment, scaling, and management of containerized applications. It provides a rich set of features for container scheduling, service discovery, load balancing, and self-healing, making it ideal for deploying and managing complex microservices architectures. Kubernetes follows a master-worker architecture, with the Kubernetes Master overseeing the cluster's operations and the Kubernetes Nodes running the containerized workloads.

To deploy and manage applications with Kubernetes, operators use the following CLI commands:

Create Kubernetes Deployment:

bashCopy code

```
kubectl create deployment myapp --image=myapp:v1
```

This command creates a Kubernetes Deployment named "myapp" using the Docker image "myapp:v1".

Scale Kubernetes Deployment:

bashCopy code

```
kubectl scale deployment myapp --replicas=3
```

This command scales the number of replicas of the "myapp" Deployment to three instances, ensuring high availability and fault tolerance.

Expose Kubernetes Service:

bashCopy code

kubectl expose deployment myapp --port=80 --type=LoadBalancer

This command exposes the "myapp" Deployment as a LoadBalancer service, allowing external traffic to access the application on port 80.

In summary, containerization technologies like Docker and Kubernetes have transformed the way software applications are developed, deployed, and managed in modern IT environments. By providing lightweight, portable environments for running applications, containers enable organizations to achieve greater agility, scalability, and resource efficiency. With Docker simplifying the process of building and running containers and Kubernetes offering advanced orchestration capabilities for managing containerized workloads at scale, businesses can embrace containerization to accelerate their digital transformation journey and stay competitive in today's fast-paced market.

Containerization has revolutionized the deployment and management of Big Data applications by providing a lightweight, portable, and scalable infrastructure. However, managing large-scale containerized Big Data deployments can be challenging without the right orchestration tools. Next, we explore various orchestration tools designed specifically for managing containerized Big Data applications, including Apache Mesos, Kubernetes, Docker Swarm, and Apache YARN.

Apache Mesos:

Apache Mesos is an open-source cluster manager that provides efficient resource isolation and sharing across distributed applications. Mesos abstracts CPU, memory, storage, and other compute resources, allowing multiple frameworks, including Big Data frameworks like Apache Hadoop and Apache Spark, to run concurrently on the same cluster. Mesos offers fault tolerance, scalability, and dynamic resource allocation, making it suitable for deploying and managing containerized Big Data applications at scale.

To deploy containerized Big Data applications with Mesos, operators use the following CLI commands:

Install and Start Mesos Master:

bashCopy code

```
mesos-master --ip=<master_ip> --work_dir=/var/lib/mesos
```

This command starts the Mesos Master daemon on the specified IP address with the default working directory.

Install and Start Mesos Agent:

bashCopy code

```
mesos-agent --master=<master_ip>:5050 --work_dir=/var/lib/mesos
```

This command starts the Mesos Agent daemon and connects it to the specified Mesos Master.

Submit Mesos Framework:

bashCopy code

```
mesos-execute --master=<master_ip>:5050 --name=my-framework --command="echo hello"
```

This command submits a Mesos framework named "my-framework" with a simple command to print "hello".

Kubernetes:

Kubernetes, as discussed in the previous chapter, is a powerful container orchestration platform that excels at managing containerized applications, including Big Data workloads. Kubernetes provides features such as auto-scaling, rolling updates, service discovery, and load balancing, making it an ideal choice for deploying and managing containerized Big Data applications in production environments.

To deploy and manage containerized Big Data applications with Kubernetes, operators use Kubernetes resources like Deployments, Services, and PersistentVolumes. Here's a brief overview:

Create Kubernetes Deployment:

bashCopy code

```
kubectl create deployment my-bigdata-app --image=my-bigdata-image:v1
```

This command creates a Kubernetes Deployment named "my-bigdata-app" using the specified Docker image.

Expose Kubernetes Service:

bashCopy code

```
kubectl expose deployment my-bigdata-app --port=8080 --target-port=8080 --type=LoadBalancer
```

This command exposes the "my-bigdata-app" Deployment as a LoadBalancer service, allowing external access to the application on port 8080.

Scale Kubernetes Deployment:

bashCopy code

kubectl scale deployment my-bigdata-app --replicas=3

This command scales the number of replicas of the "my-bigdata-app" Deployment to three instances, ensuring high availability and scalability.

Docker Swarm:

Docker Swarm is a native clustering and orchestration tool for Docker containers, providing similar features to Kubernetes but with a simpler architecture. Docker Swarm allows operators to create and manage a cluster of Docker hosts, known as a Swarm, and deploy containerized applications across the cluster seamlessly.

To deploy containerized Big Data applications with Docker Swarm, operators use Docker CLI commands along with Docker Compose files to define the application stack. Here's a basic example:

Initialize Docker Swarm:

bashCopy code

docker swarm init --advertise-addr <manager_ip>

This command initializes Docker Swarm on the host and designates it as the Swarm manager.

Deploy Docker Stack:

bashCopy code

docker stack deploy -c docker-compose.yml my-bigdata-stack

This command deploys a Docker stack named "my-bigdata-stack" using the definitions specified in the docker-compose.yml file.

View Docker Stack Services:

bashCopy code

docker stack services my-bigdata-stack

This command displays the services running in the Docker stack, including their status and ports.

Apache YARN:

Apache YARN (Yet Another Resource Negotiator) is a resource management and job scheduling framework for Hadoop, designed to enable a variety of data processing engines to run on a shared cluster. While YARN is not specifically designed for container orchestration, it can be extended to support containerized workloads through projects like Apache Hadoop YARN Docker integration.

To deploy containerized Big Data applications with Apache YARN, operators typically use YARN's ResourceManager and NodeManager daemons to manage and execute containerized tasks within the Hadoop cluster. While there are no specific CLI commands for deploying containerized applications in YARN, operators can leverage Docker images and YARN's resource management capabilities to run containerized tasks alongside traditional Hadoop jobs.

Chapter 9: Real-time Data Processing

In today's fast-paced digital world, where data is generated at an unprecedented rate, traditional batch processing methods are no longer sufficient for real-time data analysis and decision-making. Stream processing paradigms have emerged as a powerful solution to address this need, enabling organizations to process and analyze data streams in real time. Next, we explore two prominent stream processing frameworks: Apache Kafka and Apache Flink.

Apache Kafka:

Apache Kafka is an open-source distributed event streaming platform designed for building real-time data pipelines and streaming applications. It was originally developed by LinkedIn and later open-sourced as a part of the Apache Software Foundation. Kafka provides a distributed, fault-tolerant, and scalable architecture for handling high-throughput data streams.

To deploy and configure Apache Kafka, operators use the following CLI commands:

Download and Extract Kafka:

bashCopy code

```
wget https://downloads.apache.org/kafka/<version>/kafka_<version>.tgz tar -xzf kafka_<version>.tgz cd kafka_<version>
```

This command downloads the Kafka binary distribution, extracts it, and navigates to the Kafka directory.

Start ZooKeeper:

bashCopy code

```
bin/zookeeper-server-start.sh
config/zookeeper.properties
```

This command starts the ZooKeeper server, which is required for Kafka's coordination and metadata management.

Start Kafka Broker:

bashCopy code

```
bin/kafka-server-start.sh config/server.properties
```

This command starts the Kafka broker, which handles message storage, replication, and communication with producers and consumers.

Create Kafka Topic:

bashCopy code

```
bin/kafka-topics.sh --create --topic my-topic --bootstrap-server localhost:9092 --partitions 1 --replication-factor 1
```

This command creates a Kafka topic named "my-topic" with one partition and one replication factor.

Apache Flink:

Apache Flink is an open-source stream processing framework that provides powerful capabilities for event-driven applications and real-time analytics. Flink is designed to handle both batch and stream processing workloads, offering low-latency processing, exactly-once semantics, and efficient state management.

To deploy and configure Apache Flink, operators use the following CLI commands:

Download and Extract Flink:

bashCopy code

```
wget https://www.apache.org/dyn/closer.lua/flink/flink-<version>/flink-<version>-bin-scala_2.11.tgz tar -xzf flink-<version>-bin-scala_2.11.tgz cd flink-<version>
```

This command downloads the Flink binary distribution, extracts it, and navigates to the Flink directory.

Start Flink Cluster:

bashCopy code

```
./bin/start-cluster.sh
```

This command starts the Flink cluster with a single JobManager and TaskManager instance.

Submit Flink Job:

bashCopy code

```
./bin/flink run -m <jobmanager_host>:8081 examples/streaming/WordCount.jar
```

This command submits a Flink job to the cluster for execution. In this example, we run the WordCount example job.

Stream Processing Paradigms in Action:

Once Apache Kafka and Apache Flink are deployed and configured, organizations can leverage these stream processing paradigms to build real-time data processing pipelines and applications. Apache Kafka serves as the data ingestion and messaging backbone, enabling the reliable and scalable transport of data streams between producers and consumers. Apache Flink, on the other hand, provides the computational engine for processing and analyzing the data streams in real time, allowing for complex event processing, windowing, and aggregation.

For example, organizations can use Apache Kafka to ingest data from various sources such as IoT devices, web servers, or sensors, and then process this data in real time using Apache Flink to detect anomalies, perform predictive maintenance, or generate real-time insights. The combination of Kafka and Flink enables organizations to unlock the full potential of their streaming data, driving innovation and competitive advantage in today's data-driven landscape.

Real-time data processing has become increasingly essential for businesses across various industries to gain timely insights, respond to events promptly, and make informed decisions. Next, we explore the use cases and architectures for real-time data processing, focusing on how organizations leverage streaming technologies to address their specific requirements.

Use Cases:

Fraud Detection: Financial institutions use real-time data processing to detect fraudulent transactions as they occur. By analyzing transaction data in real time, anomalies and suspicious patterns can be identified promptly, allowing for immediate action to mitigate fraud risks.

IoT Analytics: Internet of Things (IoT) devices generate vast amounts of data continuously. Real-time data processing enables organizations to analyze sensor data, monitor device health, and detect anomalies in real time. This is crucial for industries such as manufacturing, healthcare, and smart cities.

Dynamic Pricing: E-commerce platforms and ride-sharing services utilize real-time data processing to adjust prices dynamically based on demand, competitor pricing, and other relevant factors. By analyzing market data in real time, these businesses can optimize pricing strategies and maximize revenue.

Social Media Analytics: Social media platforms analyze real-time user interactions, sentiment, and trends to deliver personalized content, targeted advertisements, and timely responses to user inquiries. Real-time data processing enables these platforms to stay relevant and engaging to their users.

Supply Chain Optimization: Real-time data processing helps organizations optimize supply chain operations by monitoring inventory levels, tracking shipments in real time, and predicting demand fluctuations. This enables them to make timely adjustments to inventory, transportation, and distribution processes.

Architectures:

Lambda Architecture: The Lambda architecture combines batch and stream processing to provide both real-time and batch views of data. It typically consists of three layers: the batch layer for storing and processing historical data, the speed layer for processing real-time data, and the serving layer for serving queries and results.

Kappa Architecture: The Kappa architecture simplifies the Lambda architecture by using a single stream processing layer for both real-time and batch processing. It eliminates the need for maintaining separate codebases for batch and stream processing, resulting in a more streamlined and scalable architecture.

Microservices Architecture: In a microservices architecture, real-time data processing functionalities are implemented as independent, decoupled services that communicate via lightweight protocols such as HTTP or messaging queues. This architecture enables greater flexibility, scalability, and agility in deploying and managing real-time data processing applications.

Cloud-native Architecture: Cloud providers offer a wide range of managed services for real-time data processing, such as Amazon Kinesis, Google Cloud Dataflow, and Azure Stream Analytics. These services abstract the underlying infrastructure complexity and provide scalable, reliable, and cost-effective solutions for real-time data processing in the cloud.

Deployment:

Deploying Apache Kafka: To deploy Apache Kafka, organizations can use containerization technologies such as Docker and Kubernetes to create scalable and resilient Kafka clusters. They can use Kubernetes operators like Strimzi to automate the deployment, configuration, and management of Kafka clusters on Kubernetes.

Deploying Apache Flink: Apache Flink can be deployed on various infrastructure environments, including on-premises data centers, cloud platforms, and Kubernetes clusters. Organizations can use tools like Apache Ambari, Apache Mesos, or Kubernetes operators to deploy and manage Flink clusters efficiently.

Cloud-based Real-time Data Processing: Cloud providers offer fully managed services for real-time data processing, eliminating the need for organizations to manage infrastructure and scalability concerns. By leveraging services like Amazon Kinesis, Google Cloud Dataflow, or Azure Stream Analytics, organizations can focus on building real-time data processing applications without worrying about infrastructure management.

In summary, real-time data processing plays a vital role in enabling organizations to extract actionable insights from streaming data sources. By understanding the use cases, architectures, and deployment strategies for real-time data processing, organizations can harness the power of streaming technologies to drive innovation, improve operational efficiency, and stay competitive in today's fast-paced business environment.

Chapter 10: Case Studies in Big Data Architecture

Case Study 1: Implementing a Scalable Data Warehouse
Introduction: In this case study, we will explore the implementation of a scalable data warehouse solution for a fictional e-commerce company, "TechTrend." As TechTrend experiences rapid growth in its customer base and product offerings, the need for a scalable data warehouse becomes paramount to support the increasing volume of data and analytics requirements.

Business Requirements: TechTrend aims to analyze customer behavior, sales trends, and product performance to make data-driven decisions and enhance the overall customer experience. The key business requirements for the scalable data warehouse solution include:

Scalability: The solution should be able to handle the growing volume of data and accommodate future expansion without compromising performance.

Performance: The data warehouse should provide fast query response times to enable real-time analytics and reporting.

Flexibility: The solution should support both structured and unstructured data types and allow for easy integration with various data sources.

Cost-effectiveness: While scalability and performance are essential, the solution should also be cost-effective to ensure optimal resource utilization.

Architecture Design: Based on the business requirements, the architecture for the scalable data warehouse solution is designed as follows:

Cloud-based Infrastructure: Leveraging the scalability and flexibility of cloud computing, the data warehouse will be deployed on a cloud platform such as Amazon Web Services (AWS), Microsoft Azure, or Google Cloud Platform (GCP).

Distributed Storage: To handle large volumes of data, the data warehouse will utilize distributed storage technologies such as Amazon S3, Azure Blob Storage, or Google Cloud Storage (GCS). These storage solutions offer virtually unlimited scalability and durability at a low cost.

Distributed Processing: For data processing and analytics, the solution will employ distributed processing frameworks such as Apache Hadoop, Apache Spark, or Google BigQuery. These frameworks support parallel processing of data across multiple nodes, enabling high-performance analytics at scale.

Data Modeling: The data warehouse will employ a dimensional modeling approach, organizing data into fact tables and dimension tables to facilitate efficient querying and analysis. Tools like Apache Hive, Amazon Redshift, or Snowflake will be used for data modeling and schema design.

Deployment: To deploy the scalable data warehouse solution for TechTrend, the following steps can be followed:

Provision Cloud Infrastructure: Using the CLI commands provided by the chosen cloud platform (e.g., AWS CLI,

Azure CLI, or GCP CLI), provision the necessary compute and storage resources for deploying the data warehouse.

Set Up Distributed Storage: Create buckets or containers in the chosen cloud storage service (e.g., Amazon S3, Azure Blob Storage, or Google Cloud Storage) to store the data. Use CLI commands to configure access controls and encryption settings for data security.

Install and Configure Distributed Processing Framework: Install the selected distributed processing framework (e.g., Apache Hadoop, Apache Spark, or Google BigQuery) on the provisioned compute resources. Configure the cluster settings, including the number of nodes, memory allocation, and network configurations, using CLI commands or configuration files.

Data Ingestion: Use ETL (Extract, Transform, Load) tools or scripts to ingest data from various sources into the distributed storage layer. Use CLI commands to schedule data ingestion jobs and monitor their progress.

Data Modeling and Querying: Define the data model and schema for the data warehouse using tools like Apache Hive, Amazon Redshift, or Snowflake. Write SQL queries or use BI (Business Intelligence) tools to query the data warehouse and generate insights.

Monitoring and Optimization: Monitor the performance and resource utilization of the data warehouse using monitoring tools provided by the cloud platform or third-party solutions. Use CLI commands to scale resources up or down based on workload requirements and optimize query performance.

By implementing a scalable data warehouse solution on a cloud platform, TechTrend can effectively manage and analyze large volumes of data to gain valuable insights into customer behavior, sales trends, and product performance. The cloud-based architecture provides the flexibility and scalability needed to support TechTrend's growth trajectory while ensuring cost-effectiveness and high performance.

Case Study 2: Building a Real-time Analytics Platform

Introduction: In this case study, we will explore the development of a real-time analytics platform for a fictitious social media company, "SocialSphere." As SocialSphere experiences exponential growth in user activity and data generation, the need for real-time analytics capabilities becomes critical to gain actionable insights and enhance user engagement.

Business Requirements: SocialSphere aims to analyze user interactions, content trends, and engagement metrics in real-time to optimize content delivery, personalize user experiences, and identify emerging trends. The key business requirements for the real-time analytics platform include:

Real-time Data Processing: The platform should be capable of processing and analyzing streaming data in real-time to provide timely insights and responses.

Scalability: As user activity and data volume increase, the platform should scale horizontally to handle the growing workload without sacrificing performance.

Fault Tolerance: The platform should be resilient to failures and ensure high availability to prevent data loss and service downtime.

Integration with Existing Systems: The platform should seamlessly integrate with SocialSphere's existing infrastructure and data sources, including social media APIs, databases, and third-party services.

Interactive Dashboards: The platform should provide interactive dashboards and visualizations to enable users to explore and analyze data dynamically.

Architecture Design: Based on the business requirements, the architecture for the real-time analytics platform is designed as follows:

Stream Processing Engine: The platform will utilize a stream processing engine such as Apache Kafka, Apache Flink, or Amazon Kinesis to ingest, process, and analyze streaming data in real-time. These engines provide fault-tolerant and scalable processing capabilities for handling high-throughput data streams.

Microservices Architecture: The platform will be designed as a set of loosely coupled microservices deployed in containerized environments using Docker and orchestrated with Kubernetes. This architecture enables scalability, fault isolation, and independent deployment of services.

Data Storage: Processed data will be stored in scalable and distributed storage systems such as Apache Cassandra, Amazon DynamoDB, or Google Cloud Bigtable. These NoSQL databases provide high throughput and low-latency access to data, ideal for real-time analytics workloads.

Real-time Dashboards: Interactive dashboards and visualizations will be built using tools like Apache Superset, Grafana, or Tableau. These tools allow users to explore data in real-time and gain insights through intuitive visualizations and charts.

Deployment: To deploy the real-time analytics platform for SocialSphere, the following steps can be followed:

Provision Cloud Infrastructure: Using the CLI commands provided by the chosen cloud provider (e.g., AWS CLI, Azure CLI, or GCP CLI), provision the necessary compute, storage, and networking resources for deploying the platform.

Set Up Stream Processing Engine: Deploy the chosen stream processing engine (e.g., Apache Kafka, Apache Flink, or Amazon Kinesis) on the provisioned compute resources. Configure topics, partitions, and consumer groups using CLI commands or configuration files.

Containerize Microservices: Containerize each microservice using Docker and define Dockerfiles to specify dependencies and runtime configurations. Use CLI commands to build and push Docker images to a container registry like Docker Hub or Amazon ECR.

Orchestrate with Kubernetes: Deploy Kubernetes clusters using CLI commands provided by the cloud provider or Kubernetes distributions like Minikube or kops. Use YAML configuration files to define Kubernetes resources such as deployments, services, and ingress rules.

Configure Data Storage: Set up and configure the chosen data storage systems (e.g., Apache Cassandra, Amazon DynamoDB, or Google Cloud Bigtable) using CLI commands or management consoles. Define keyspaces, tables, and indexes as needed to store and retrieve data. Develop Real-time Dashboards: Use CLI commands or web interfaces to provision virtual machines or containers for hosting the dashboarding tools (e.g., Apache Superset, Grafana, or Tableau Server). Configure data sources and create interactive dashboards and visualizations to monitor key metrics and KPIs.

Test and Monitor: Conduct comprehensive testing of the deployed platform to ensure functionality, performance, and reliability. Monitor system metrics, resource utilization, and data pipelines using monitoring tools provided by the cloud platform or third-party solutions.

By building a real-time analytics platform using scalable and fault-tolerant technologies, SocialSphere can effectively analyze streaming data to gain actionable insights and drive business decisions in real-time. The cloud-native architecture, microservices design, and container orchestration enable agility, scalability, and resilience, positioning SocialSphere for success in the dynamic landscape of social media analytics.

Conclusion

In summary, the "Big Data: Statistics, Data Mining, Analytics, and Pattern Learning" book bundle offers a comprehensive journey into the vast and evolving landscape of big data and analytics. Across four distinct volumes, readers are guided through the fundamental principles, advanced techniques, and architectural considerations essential for navigating the complexities of big data processing and analysis.

In "Big Data Fundamentals," readers are introduced to the foundational concepts of data analytics and processing, providing a solid understanding of the underlying principles and technologies driving the big data revolution. From data collection to storage and analysis, this book equips readers with the knowledge needed to harness the power of data for informed decision-making.

"Data Mining Techniques" delves deeper into the exploration of patterns and insights within big data, offering a comprehensive overview of data mining algorithms, methodologies, and best practices. Through practical examples and case studies, readers gain insights into the application of data mining techniques across various industries and domains.

"Advanced Data Science" elevates readers' understanding of big data analysis by delving into the realm of machine learning. From regression analysis to clustering and neural networks, this book explores the intricate algorithms and methodologies that drive predictive modeling and pattern recognition in big data environments.

Finally, "Big Data Architecture and Scalability" addresses the critical considerations involved in designing robust systems for enterprise big data solutions. By exploring architectural patterns, scalability techniques, and fault tolerance mechanisms, readers gain insights into building resilient and scalable big data platforms capable of meeting the demands of modern enterprises.

Collectively, these four volumes serve as an indispensable resource for professionals, academics, and enthusiasts seeking to navigate the complexities of big data analytics. Whether you are embarking on your journey into the world of big data or seeking to deepen your expertise, this book bundle provides a comprehensive and insightful guide to mastering the intricacies of big data analytics and pattern learning.